JONATHAN'S

JOURNEY

JONATHAN'S JOURNEY

KATHERINE BELL

THOMAS NELSON PUBLISHERS
Nashville • Atlanta • London • Vancouver

fic

Published in Nashville, Tennessee, by Thomas Nelson, Inc., Publishers, and distributed in Canada by Word Communications, Ltd., Richmond, British Columbia.

Unless otherwise noted scripture quotations are from The Holy Bible: NEW INTERNATIONAL VERSION, Copyright © 1978 by the New York International Bible Society. Used by permission of Zondervan Bible Publishers.

Scripture quotations noted NKJV are from the New King James Version. Copyright © 1979, 1980, 1982, Thomas Nelson, Inc., Publishers.

All song lyrics are public domain unless otherwise indicated.

Lyrics of the hymn *Great is The Faithfulness*, by Thomas O. Chisolm, © 1923 and 1951, are used by permission from Hope Publishing Company, Carol Stream, Illinois, 60188.

Illustrations by Steven Miller.

Library of Congress Cataloging-in-Publication Data

Bell, Katherine
    Jonathan's journey/Katherine Bell.
       p.   cm.
    "A Jan Dennis Book"
    ISBN 0-7852-8040-5
    1. Handicapped children—Fiction. 2. Jesus Christ—Fiction. I. Title
PS3552.E516J66 1992
813'.54—dc20   94-8899
                                                CIP

Printed in the United States of America

1 2 3 4 5 6 — 99 98 97 96 95 94

Jesus said,

"Let the little children come to me,

and do not hinder them,

for the kingdom of heaven

belongs to such as these."

—Matthew 19:14

For from Him

and through Him

and to Him are all things.

To Him

be the glory forever!

Amen.

—Romans 11:36

Acknowledgments

Special thanks are in order to everyone who helped and encouraged me with this book:

... to my husband Craig—for your constant and unwavering support. I love you!

... to the Klentzmans—Rick and Mary, Kimberly, Matthew, Jill, Mark, Jonathan, and Andrew—and to Katherine Halliday;

... to Steve Miller, and to Donna, Christy, and Ben;

... to my church family at Bethany Bible Church;

... to Frank Simon, David Lines, Dennis Hartwick, and Clarence Mingee;

... to Sara, Marvin, Ben, and Amy Effa;

... and a very special thanks to my pastor, Dr. Marvin J. Effa. Marv, Craig and I could never adequately express our love and appreciation for you. The Lord has used you immeasurably in our lives. Thank you for showing me what it means to love the Lord!

Table of Contents

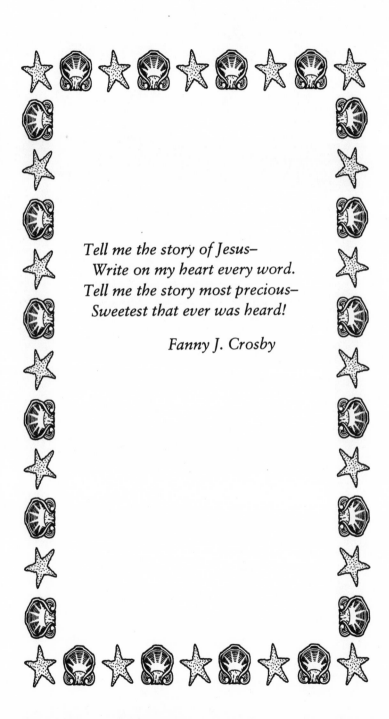

Tell me the story of Jesus—
Write on my heart every word.
Tell me the story most precious—
Sweetest that ever was heard!

Fanny J. Crosby

1

A Visitor in the Night

God made Jonathan different.

Even before he was born, he was not like other children. "Things are not right this time," the doctor told his parents sadly, shaking his head. "You are carrying identical twins, but I can only hear one heartbeat."

And the doctor was right. When Jonathan was born, his twin brother had already died. And although Jonathan did live, he was very different from his four brothers and sisters.

His head was very small, and his muscles were stiff and uncontrollable. As he grew, he did not learn to talk, or to crawl, or to feed himself. He could not sit up, even with help, because his back was stiff and tended to arch backwards on its own. Even his hands were constantly clenched and useless, and he could not grasp things like other babies.

So his mother and father fed him, carried him, talked to him, and sang to him, and did for him all the things he could not do for himself.

And they loved him fiercely. Through all the trials and difficulties, they thanked God for their special little boy, and for his brother who would be waiting to meet them someday in heaven.

Although Jonathan knew he was different, he did not understand why. Most of the time, it did not matter—his family loved him, and he was happy. But sometimes he wondered.

He loved to listen to his sisters, Kimberly and Jill, talk and giggle together. He always smiled and laughed at the sounds of their cheerful voices, especially when they spoke to him in their loving way. "Hey, Jonathan," they would say. "Come on, Jonathan, smile for us—can you smile for us? Just look at that big smile!" But he could not understand what they were saying. And although he wanted to answer them, he did not know how to make the words.

He loved to play with his brothers, Matthew and Mark. But they ran around the house and yard on their legs, and used their hands to hold and throw things. *How do they do it?* he wondered. *Why can't I?*

Almost every day, Kimberly would carry him to the piano and hold him in her lap while she practiced—sometimes for hours at a time. Jonathan loved the music and the attention, and he would sit there with her for as long as his stiff, uncooperative body would allow, listening enraptured, and making small, happy sounds as if begging her to play on and on and on.

But best of all was when the entire family would stand together and sing. His mother or Kim would sit at the piano, his father would play his guitar, and sometimes one of his brothers would even join in on the drums. And they would lift their voices together, each of them singing a different part, until the harmonies blended together into that wonderful sound that carried Jonathan away to secret magical places.

And when they sang, one of them would always hold him—right there in the middle of it all, wrapped in joy and tingling with inner delight. How he wished he could sing with them!

He loved to be held—the feel of his father's arms around him, his mother's familiar softness as she cradled him, his grandma's fond caress on his cheek—these were the best feelings in the world.

Next to their music, he loved their voices best, gently calling his name, speaking to him in that quiet tone that he knew was just for him. And he especially loved it when they said to him—over and over—the four words that he knew, the only four words that he was sure he understood:

"Jonathan, I love you—I love you, Jonathan . . . I love you!"

⊕

One night, Jonathan did not feel very well. He could not go to sleep, and he cried when his mother set him down. So she took him in her arms, and for a while she held him and talked to him, walked with him, and murmured quiet words of comfort.

But by now he was almost five years old, and at forty pounds had become almost too much for her to carry. So at last, she sank into an old overstuffed recliner, laid his head against her chest, and as they rocked together, began to sing softly . . .

Baby's boat's a silver moon, sailing through the sky—
Sailing o'er the seas asleep while the stars go by;
Sail, Baby, sail—out among the seas,
Only don't forget to sail . . . back again to me.

It felt good to snuggle up against her. She sang on, her low voice and the soothing familiar melodies finally lulling him to sleep . . .

Jesus loves me, this I know,
for the Bible tells me so,
Little ones to Him belong—
they are weak, but He is strong . . .

Finally, Jonathan slept. His mother did not want to wake him by moving, so before long, she slept, too.

It was several hours later when Jonathan suddenly woke up. Someone had called his name.

He opened his eyes and listened.

It had not been his mother's voice—she was asleep, and the house was quiet. It was very late, and he could see through the window that it was dark outside.

But the room was flooded with light.

"Jonathan," he heard again. Then he saw a man standing in the doorway. And the soft glow that soothed the darkness came from his face.

The man came into the room and leaned over Jonathan. His bearded face was quiet and beautiful. His eyes were kind and full of laughter, and he gazed at Jonathan with a smile so full of love that the boy immediately wanted to reach out to him. But he could not. Jonathan could not remember ever having seen him before. But somehow, he was not a stranger.

Who are you? Jonathan wanted to ask, but he did not know the words, or how to speak them.

The man began to stroke Jonathan's cheek, and his touch was even softer and kinder than Mommy's. His face was not familiar, but it was perfect in every way—except that he had long, deep scars all over his forehead.

He loves me, Jonathan knew.

More than Kimberly and Matthew? he wondered.

Yes.

More than Jill and Mark?

Yes, more than Jill and Mark.

But not more than Daddy and Mommy. No one could love him more than Daddy and Mommy.

But as he stared at that beautiful, scarred face, he knew somehow . . . *No one in the whole world loves me more than you do . . .*

But who are you?

The man seemed to know how desperately Jonathan longed to speak to him. He stretched out his hand and gently traced the outline of Jonathan's mouth. Then he spoke. "Talk to me, Jonathan," he said softly.

Instantly, the words came to Jonathan's tongue. "Who are you?" he asked, listening in wonder to the sound of his own voice.

"My name is Jesus," the man replied simply. "I made you."

"Jesus?" Jonathan said. "I've heard that name before. Mommy sings about you all the time." He frowned in thought. "But how does she know you? I've never seen you here before."

"Your mommy has known me for many years," the

man replied. "We speak together often. But tonight, I came to see you."

"Why?"

"Because I have many things to tell you," he smiled. "Get up and come with me."

Jonathan's face suddenly clouded with worry. "But I can't. Mommy has to carry me everywhere I go, and she's asleep."

The man laughed, then gently lifted Jonathan out of his mother's arms and set him on his own feet. Jonathan looked about him in confusion, then suddenly realized that he was standing. His feet felt strange, but strong and good, and the world looked wonderfully different from this angle.

The man stepped back and held out his hand to Jonathan. "Walk to me," he said.

Jonathan did. He was surprised at how simple it was. He took the man's hand and looked up at him with growing wonder.

"Let's go for a walk," Jesus suggested.

Jonathan hesitated. "But what about Mommy?" he asked.

Jesus looked at Jonathan's mother. She had not awakened at their voices or when Jesus had taken Jonathan from her arms. Her face showed exhaustion, even in sleep, and was creased with lines of concern and fatigue. He let go of Jonathan and took her hand in his. Kissing her forehead softly, he whispered to her, "Don't be troubled, Mary—all is well."

Even before he had finished speaking, Jonathan saw her tense face relax. Then she curled up comfortably in the chair and fell far beyond dreams into that deepest kind of sleep.

"Now we can go," Jesus said, taking Jonathan's hand again. "Your mother has worked hard. We'll let her rest."

"Okay," said Jonathan. Together, they walked hand in hand to the front door. Both of them seemed to understand that Mommy might wake up if they unlocked and opened the door, so instead, they walked through it and into the night.

The spacious firmament on high
  With all the blue ethereal sky,
And spangled heavens, a shining frame,
  Their great Original proclaim.

The unwearied sun, from day to day,
  Does his Creator's power display;
And publishes to every land
  The work of an almighty hand.

Soon as the evening shades prevail
  The moon takes up the wondrous tale;
And nightly to the listening earth
  Repeats the story of her birth;

While all the stars that 'round her burn,
  And all the planets in their turn...
Forever singing as they shine,
  "The hand that made us is divine!"

Joseph Addison
based on Psalm 19

2

Made for Himself

"This isn't *my* yard," Jonathan said suddenly and looked back toward the house.

It was gone. In its place was a country gravel road. The sky was veiled in gray clouds, and there were no lights anywhere. Nearby, the black form of a cow, almost invisible against the dark sky, gazed sleepily at them through a barbed wire fence while her calf dozed undisturbed at her side. But beyond them, Jonathan could see very little. It was quite dark.

Jonathan tugged at the man's hand. "Where are we, Jesus?" he asked.

"At your grandma's farm," Jesus replied. "Do you remember coming here?"

Until he spoke, Jonathan did not remember. But now it was so clear. Of course! Grandma's house—the squeals and giggles of all his brothers and sisters and cousins playing together; the smells of roast turkey; and the deep green pine tree covered with flickering colored lights and bright packages. And music—so much music, all the time! He smiled at the memory.

Jesus smiled, too, as if he knew what Jonathan was thinking about, and also remembered it well.

"Grandma's house!" Jonathan sighed happily. "Yes, I remember! Are we going to see Grandma now? Does she know you, too?"

"Yes," he replied. "She does. But we are not going to see her tonight. I brought you here to show you the stars in my heavens."

"The stars?" Jonathan asked curiously. "I don't see any stars."

Jesus looked upwards absently, as if only just noticing the heavy blanket of clouds that hid the sky. He reached out with his hand and drew them back in a single sweeping motion, as easily as if pulling aside the drapes on the back door.

Jonathan gasped. The dark country sky suddenly sparkled with hundreds and thousands of tiny, twinkling lights. They were small, each of them so tiny, almost invisible. But together, they were bright enough to cast faint shadows on the lawn. The longer Jonathan watched, the more he could see, until there were more stars than sky.

"Those are my stars," Jesus said. "I made them, and set them in the heavens for you to see."

"You made them?" Jonathan breathed in a whisper.

"Yes."

"When?"

The man drew Jonathan up in his arms and held him closely. "I'll tell you about it," he said, and together they watched the night sky.

"It was many years ago," he began, "when I made this world. I took six days to do it.

"First I made light and dark. Then I made the heavens, the oceans, the dry land, and all the plants and trees. I made the sun, and the moon, and all the stars . . . "

"Those stars?" Jonathan pointed.

"Those very ones," Jesus replied. "Then the fish, and the birds, and all the animals."

Jonathan was thrilled. At last, a story—told just for *him*, not overheard. And he was understanding it! He joined in enthusiastically. "When did you make me?" he demanded happily.

Jesus laughed. "Not until much later. But at the end of that first week, last of all, I made the very first man, so that he could take care of all the good things that I had made. And on the seventh day, I rested and enjoyed my creation."

"You made the first man?" Jonathan repeated, trying to sort it all out. He had seen his sisters make things before with paper and scissors and glue. But to make a man? He could not imagine it. "How did you do that?" he asked.

Jesus paused, then in answer, he knelt beside the gravel road and motioned for Jonathan to sit beside him. He said nothing but gathered up some dust in his hands, and molded it quietly with his fingers. As Jonathan watched, a tiny figure took shape almost immediately.

What was Jesus doing? Fascinated, Jonathan watched in enchantment while Jesus formed little hands and feet, hair and ears, and carved tiny features on the little face with his fingertips.

It was too wonderful to watch from even a short distance, so Jonathan leaned closer, peering anxiously at the mysterious figure in Jesus' hands. But before the little boy could even catch his breath, the tiny figure was complete.

"It's a little girl!" Jonathan gasped, staring at the doll-like form.

He had never seen such a beautiful creature. Every feature was perfect, from the impossibly fine lashes on her closed eyes, to the tiny red lips, and the long golden hair that drifted around her cheeks in the light breeze. Her arms and fingers were long and graceful, and she looked as though she might rise up and dance in the starlight out of the sheer joy of her own beauty.

But she lay still, not even breathing.

With great hesitation, Jonathan reached out and rested his fingers on Jesus' hand but could not bring himself to touch the motionless figure.

He was almost afraid to ask. "Why doesn't she get up?" he whispered.

"There is no life in her yet," Jesus explained.

"Yet?" Jonathan asked. "Where will it come from?"

"From me," Jesus answered. "*All* life comes from me. Watch!"

Then he leaned over the clay figure and blew softly on her face. As he did, the little eyes opened, and when she saw him, she leaped gracefully to her feet and gazed up with adoration into her creator's eyes.

"Lord Jesus!" she greeted him in a musical voice, full of awe and worship. "Beloved Son of the Most High God!"

Jonathan stared, speechless, as she continued. "How majestic is Your name, my Lord and God, Creator of all things—worthy of all glory and honor and power . . . !" Then, it seemed, her words failed her, and she simply stood with upraised arms gazing into his face, her eyes alight with joy.

At last she also noticed the astonished little boy at their side and faced him with a dazzling smile. "Hello, Jonathan," she greeted him. "How handsome you are tonight!"

"Who . . . who are you?!" he stammered in reply.

The tiny girl's laugh was like a silver bell. "I don't know," she said. "My Lord has not named me yet. But I can tell you of Him," she continued eagerly. She lifted her face towards the sky, and Jonathan's eyes followed her outstretched hands upwards to the brilliant, starry heavens.

"Look!" she exclaimed. "You and I could never count them, but He brings them out one by one and calls each of them by name! He put the moon there to shine with them at night and the sun to light up the day. He made *everything* in heaven and on the earth—everything you see and everything you do not see."

"What do you mean—everything I do not see?" Jonathan asked. "I can see everything you are showing me now—the stars and the moon . . . "

"Oh, but there is so much more!" she exclaimed, glancing at Jesus. He nodded to her in reply and said, "Open your eyes, Jonathan, and look around you."

And when Jonathan looked again, he gasped in astonishment. The three of them were not alone, as he had thought. Seven shining white creatures—like tall winged men in robes of pure white—stood nearby. Their giant golden wings were outstretched, tips barely touching, forming a protective circle around the little group. Each carried a flaming sword, triumphantly raised, as if daring the approach of any enemy. But when Jesus looked at them, they laid their swords on the grass and knelt, hiding their faces from him.

As they lowered their great wings, Jonathan could see others all around them. Three stood just above him on the roof of his grandma's house, and two guarded her doors. Their swords, too, were drawn, and they lifted them high in tribute. Others surrounded his Aunt Carol's house next door, and one stood watch at the curve of the road. All of them faced Jesus and bowed their heads when he looked toward them.

In the distant hills, Jonathan could see even more of them, some mounted on bright horses, some driving flaming chariots. Even the air was thick with them, and their hovering wings formed a flickering canopy of living light over his head. Many of these also held fiery swords; but others carried slender golden trumpets, which they kept at their sides, unused and silent.

But beyond them, the heavens were filled with the greatest glory Jonathan could imagine. The blackness of night was shattered by countless thousands of these angelic hosts, each shining like the sun and holding a star cupped in his outstretched hands. When Jesus lifted his head toward them, they bowed reverently. Then, one after another, they took handfuls of starlight, casting the glowing bits toward earth until the sky was streaked with white fireworks and rained glowing offerings from heaven.

Jonathan was speechless. But the little girl stood enraptured, her arms raised high in worship and her face shining with love.

"You see!" she cried joyously to Jonathan. "All

these things, he made! They are all his! They were all made *by* him, and they were all made *for* him."

Then with the greatest of delight in her voice, she turned back to Jesus. "You have made me for yourself, also," she said eagerly, "and I will be grateful to you forever! My heart is entirely yours, and I long to serve you! What shall I do to please you best?"

"You have done well already," he smiled. "But I did not make you for this world. Go to my Father's house and wait for me there."

"I will do that, Lord," she said to him. "Will you come there soon?"

"Very soon," he assured her.

"Then I shall wait gladly," she beamed.

As she spoke, one of the creatures above them left the ranks in the air and flew swiftly to them as if he had been summoned. He held out a hand to the little girl, and she waved to Jonathan as Jesus lifted her high over his head. "Good-bye, Jonathan," she called back to him. "I will see you again someday."

Then a sudden gust of wind caught her up. And as she flew away with her guide, her silver laugh echoing toward heaven, it seemed to Jonathan that he could hear a sound like the singing of the early morning stars. Then as quickly as the hosts had appeared, they vanished. And Jonathan was again alone with Jesus under the night sky.

The little boy turned to Jesus with wide and solemn eyes. "Who were they?" he whispered.

"My servants," Jesus explained. "Messengers— armies. They are called angels."

"And you made them all?" Jonathan breathed.

"All of them," Jesus replied.

"And everything else, too? Like birds?"

"Yes."

"And trees?"

"Yes."

"My mommy and daddy, and brothers and sisters?"

"Yes."

"And the stars, too . . . "

"Yes."

Jonathan sat silently for a long moment, trying to remember something he had heard once, trying to piece together overheard conversations that he had never been able to understand before. He gazed intently at the sky.

"But Mommy said that *God* made the stars," he said finally.

"She's right," the man said.

Jonathan looked up into Jesus' eyes. "Jesus, are you God?" he asked.

"Yes."

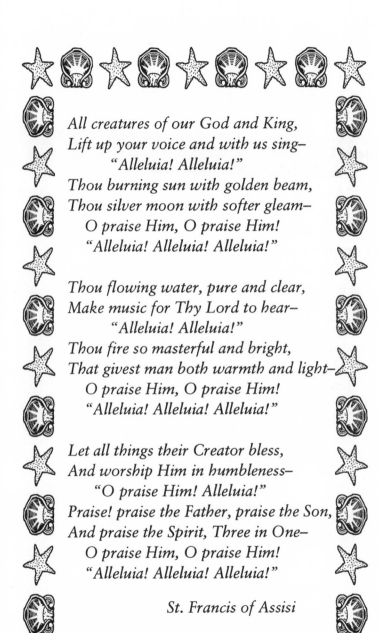

All creatures of our God and King,
Lift up your voice and with us sing–
    "Alleluia! Alleluia!"
Thou burning sun with golden beam,
Thou silver moon with softer gleam—
    O praise Him, O praise Him!
    "Alleluia! Alleluia! Alleluia!"

Thou flowing water, pure and clear,
Make music for Thy Lord to hear–
    "Alleluia! Alleluia!"
Thou fire so masterful and bright,
That givest man both warmth and light–
    O praise Him, O praise Him!
    "Alleluia! Alleluia! Alleluia!"

Let all things their Creator bless,
And worship Him in humbleness–
    "O praise Him! Alleluia!"
Praise! praise the Father, praise the Son,
And praise the Spirit, Three in One–
    O praise Him, O praise Him!
    "Alleluia! Alleluia! Alleluia!"

St. Francis of Assisi

3

Separated!

At Jesus' instruction, Jonathan took a handful of gravel from the road and scattered it in front of him. As it fell, it became grainy and damp, and as it touched the grass, it spread out in soft dunes before them. When he looked up again, they were standing on the ocean shore.

The sand felt wonderful between Jonathan's bare toes, and he squealed with delight as a hermit crab recognized its creator and scurried up to greet them.

A flock of seagulls circled about their heads, crying happily, and when Jonathan reached up toward them, one of the great birds landed softly on his outstretched hand and let him stroke its fine white feathers. Another dived at them playfully, and Jonathan leaped after it, laughing. The whole flock responded to the game, and for several breathless minutes, Jonathan ran about the beach—just like his brothers would—on his own legs. One gull came and hovered teasingly in his face. He reached out and petted it, giggling and shouting out loud with his own voice.

"I'm Jonathan!" he cried out to them. "Look at me! I'm Jonathan! Jesus made me!"

Jonathan! Jonathan! they seemed to reply. *Jesus! Yes, Jesus—yes, we know him!*

At last, they all flew away together, each in turn dipping a wing to stroke Jonathan's hair as they vanished into the night.

Jesus! their voices seemed to cry. *Jesus! Jesus!*

Delirious with happiness, Jonathan turned back. Jesus was sitting on the beach beside a small fire, watching him. There was a wonderful smell in the air.

"I ran!" Jonathan announced breathlessly, hurrying up to him. "I *ran!* Did you see me?"

"I did," he said, "and you were wonderful! Are you hungry now?"

Jonathan suddenly realized that he was.

"Come and sit beside me," Jesus said. As the boy snuggled up to his side, Jesus handed him a little piece of hot, steaming fish and a torn piece of thick, crusty bread.

Jonathan took it with surprise. He had never been able to eat solid food before. "Is this for me?" he asked.

Jesus nodded.

For a moment, Jonathan could not believe it; and he just held the food in his hands, staring at it, savoring the warmth and aroma. When he looked up again, his eyes were wet. He had thought he could be happy forever just from the memory of running with the seagulls. But now this, too!

"Thank you," was all he could manage to say.

"You are welcome, Jonathan," replied his friend.

The piece of fish was very small, and the bread looked as though it could only be a bite or two. But both were delicious, and Jonathan ate and ate and ate.

Just when he thought he was too full to eat any more, he came to the very last bite. It was just enough.

Overwhelmed with satisfaction and peace, Jonathan leaned contentedly against Jesus' side. Jesus put his arms around the little boy, and since there seemed to be no reason to hurry away, they sat quietly together by the fire for a long while, watching the starlight-crested waves crashing gently against the shore—one after another, an endless line of them, rising from the unseen reaches of the sea and coming at their master's call.

Jonathan felt wonderful—well and warm and happy and full. But Jesus' story of his creation was dancing through his mind, and he was full of questions as well.

"Jesus," he said finally, with a troubled expression, "there is something I don't understand."

"What is that?" the man replied.

"When you made the little girl, she knew you right away."

"Yes."

"But you made me, too. And I didn't know who you were when you came to see me."

"No, you didn't."

"Why not?"

"Because of something called sin."

Jonathan was not sure he liked the sound of that. "What is sin?" he asked hesitantly.

Jesus drew him closer. "That is the next part of the story I started to tell you earlier," he said, and they stared into the little red fire on the beach as he continued.

"When I made the first man, I named him Adam.

He knew us. And when I made the first woman, named Eve, to be his wife, she knew us, too."

"Did you make them the way you made the little girl?" Jonathan asked, remembering how Jesus had molded her from the dust of the road.

"I made Adam like that," Jesus replied, "but I made Eve from a bone I took out of Adam's side." He poked at Jonathan's ribs lightly, making him giggle.

"We made them like ourselves. They were good and pure and perfect. We loved them very much, and we spent a lot of time together in the beautiful new world we had made. We wanted them and their children to be with us forever. But we knew that if they ever learned how to do evil, they would become full of sin and could never be with us the way we intended them to be."

Jonathan interrupted him. "You keep saying 'we,'" he complained. "I thought *you* made them."

"I did," Jesus answered. "But there are three persons of God, and each of us had a part in creation."

"Three Gods?" Jonathan frowned.

"No," Jesus explained patiently. "One God. But there are three separate and distinct persons—my Father, Myself, and the Spirit."

"Oh," Jonathan replied, very confused. "Will I get to meet them, too?"

"By meeting me," Jesus said, "you have already met them. I am in the Father, and the Father is in me."

This was too much! Jonathan shook his head and complained, "I don't understand!"

"I know," Jesus reassured him. "But that's okay. Some things are impossible for you to understand right now. Someday you will."

Jonathan thought for a few more seconds, then gave up and returned to his original question. "But why didn't I *know* you?"

"As I said," Jesus explained, "that is because of sin."

There was that word again. "Is sin bad?" Jonathan asked. The little fire crackled suddenly, and Jonathan flinched as a shower of sparks flew up in front of him.

"Yes," Jesus replied. "Very bad. So bad that if sin came into Adam and Eve, I could not even be with them anymore."

Jonathan was appalled. "But why not?"

"Because the penalty for sin is death. God is perfect, and sin cannot come into His presence. Any creature who sins must die and be separated from me forever."

"*Forever?*" This was too much for Jonathan to comprehend, but Jesus nodded.

"Forever," he said. "But I did not want that to happen. So I made it very simple for them to remain perfect—I took all the knowledge of good and evil and put it into the fruit of one tree in their garden. They could never learn evil unless they took it from that tree.

"And I gave them only one rule: *Don't eat the fruit on that tree.* If you do, I told them, you will die."

"They didn't do it, did they?" Jonathan said hesitantly.

There was sadness in Jesus' voice as he replied, "Yes, they did."

"But why?" Jonathan cried. "Why would they do that?"

"Because I have a very evil enemy who is full of sin. He hates me and every good thing I have made. He knew that I loved these perfect people I had made for myself, so he especially hated them. He went to the garden and tried to destroy them by making them sin, too. He told Eve that I had lied to her. He told her that the fruit on that tree was very good, and that she would not die if she ate it. Instead, he told her, she would become like God.

"He was so convincing that she believed him and ate the fruit. Then she gave some to Adam, and he ate it, too."

Jonathan could not understand. "But you would never lie to them! Why did they believe *him*?"

"Because my enemy is very clever, and he tells lies that *sound* like the truth."

"Did they die?"

"Not right away. I had made them perfect, to live forever. It was many years before their bodies stopped living and became dust again, even though they had sin in them now. But we were separated instantly.

"The next day when I came to the garden, they hid from me. They had sinned, and I could not be with them as before."

"What did you do?"

"I was angry and terribly grieved because sin and death had come into my new, perfect world. I put a curse on the earth, and I made the man and woman leave the beautiful garden. You see, there was another tree there—the Tree of Life. If they ate its fruit, they would live forever with their sin. I could never again be with them, and I would lose them forever."

Jonathan was torn by the intense sadness of Jesus' voice, and the terrible grief in his face looked even more sorrowful in the dancing red shadows. "But you made them!" he insisted. "Couldn't you make them perfect again?"

"Yes," Jesus admitted. "And my Father promised them that someday he would send a Savior to take their sin away. But it would not be an easy thing to do. You see, I had given them a *choice*. They *decided* to sin. And the penalty for sin is death. *Always*, when there is sin, there has to be death to pay for it."

"Death . . .," Jonathan repeated. He thought about it for a moment, then asked carefully, "What happens to a person who dies?"

"There are two kinds of death," Jesus replied. "First, the body dies, as I have already told you. Sometimes this is very painful, sometimes less so. Sometimes death comes quickly, and other times it takes much longer. But in any case, as bad as it is, it is nothing compared to the *second* death.

"You see, I created each person with an eternal soul—the part that lives *in* his body—the part that thinks and feels and acts. The soul continues on forever, even after the body dies.

"But if there is sin in the person, his soul cannot come to be with me—he must go somewhere else. This separation from me is the second death. It is much worse, and it lasts forever."

"But if the person could not be with you," Jonathan asked fearfully, "where would he go?"

"To a terrible place!" Jesus replied emphatically. "You see, everything good comes from me. So a sinful person who could not be with me would have to go to a place which could not have any good in it at all.

"This place is horrible and frightening—a huge lake filled with fire instead of water. Since souls cannot be burned up and destroyed like their earthly bodies, they would have to stay there forever, suffering in the flames, along with my enemy and all of his followers."

Jonathan shuddered, staring into the little campfire. He tried to imagine it spread out as large as the ocean in front of them, its burning flames reaching toward the sky. Its comforting warmth seemed hotter and more threatening now, and he inched away from it.

"You couldn't want that for them," Jonathan whispered in a trembling voice.

"No, I did not!" Jesus agreed quickly. "I made them for myself, and I loved them far more than you can imagine."

"But if they died," Jonathan said, "they would be in that horrible place—you could not be with them anymore."

"That was the problem," Jesus replied. "Come with me. I'll tell you what happened."

Jesus, Lover of my soul,
  Let me to Thy bosom fly
While the nearer waters roll,
  And the tempest still is high.
Hide me, O my Savior hide,
  Till the storm of life is past!
Save into the haven guide—
  O receive my soul at last!

Plenteous grace with Thee is found,
  Grace to cover all my sin.
Let the healing streams abound—
  Make and keep me pure within.
Thou of life the fountain art,
  Freely let me take of Thee;
Spring Thou up within my heart,
  Rise to all eternity!

Charles Wesley

4

Grace on the Sea of Judgment

The little fire had burned quite low by the time they stood up to leave. Jesus spoke a single word to it, and it went out.

"Take my hand," he said to Jonathan, and the two of them walked out together onto the still waters of the ocean, following the gleaming path cast by the crescent moon on the horizon.

Somehow, Jonathan did not find it at all strange that they should walk on the surface of the ocean. The water was deliciously cool and slippery under his bare toes, and he watched with delight as schools of shining fish passed beneath them, flipping their tails in greeting to their master before swimming into the depths and out of sight.

A few of the gulls reappeared and followed them for a while, crying joyously with their shrill voices. One even perched on Jonathan's outstretched hand, balancing with its great wings unfolded while Jonathan dreamed of soaring with it through the clouds.

But in spite of all these wonders, Jonathan still reeled from the story he had heard. What a terrible thing for those first people—to be lied to, and then to sin, and then to never be able to be with Jesus again . . . He went over and over the story in his mind. The one ray of hope was this Savior that Jesus had mentioned—the Savior who would take their sin away.

He decided that he wanted to hear more about this.

But as he started to ask the question, he suddenly caught sight of something he had not noticed before. The strong hand that held his was deeply scarred— much more deeply than Jesus' face.

Looking closer, he found that the scar was even worse than it had appeared at first. With childlike curiosity, he traced its outlines with his finger, wondering, *What could have happened?*

Jesus watched him quietly, and when Jonathan looked up at him with questioning eyes, he opened his hand in answer and turned it over. The scar went all the way through to the other side.

Jonathan was so startled that he let go and immediately slipped and started to fall into the water. But Jesus caught him so quickly that only one foot got wet.

And still they walked on in silence.

Jonathan was troubled by the scar, but the more he wondered about it, the more he was afraid of what the answer might be. So when he finally broke the silence, he simply asked, "What happened to Adam and Eve after you made them leave the garden?"

"They lived for many years before they died," Jesus replied, "and they had many, many children. Their children had children, and those children had children. Soon the earth was covered with people."

"Did they know you?"

"A few did, but not very many. You see, the sin that

was in Adam and Eve went into their children, too. My enemy did not have to deceive each one of them to make them sin. They were born with sin already in them, so it was very easy for him to tempt them to sin more and more."

"All of them?"

"Every one. They became very wicked—so full of sin that all they ever thought about was the evil things they could do.

"Again, I was angry and grieved. I remembered the beautiful world I had created. I remembered making Adam from the dust and Eve from Adam's rib. I had made them perfect—like me. I had made them *for* me—to be with me, like we were those first days in the garden when we would walk together. They were my greatest creation, and I loved them.

"Then I looked at all the sinful people who were in the world now. They openly hated me, and I was very sorry that I had made them."

Jonathan was not sure he could stand to hear much more. This was terrible! Who could ever become so evil that he would hate *Jesus*? He looked up into the man's face—its light was brighter than even the stars and moon together. And while Jonathan had never been without the care and love of his family, *that* love paled in comparison to the love he saw in Jesus' eyes. And this hand that was holding him safely above the water—this very hand had made the stars . . .

Hate *Jesus*? He could not imagine even one person who could, much less a whole world.

"So . . . what did you do?"

By now, they had walked very far from shore. Jesus stopped, and motioned for Jonathan to look around.

There was nothing but water as far as they could see in every direction. The beach was lost over the horizon, and even the gulls had not ventured so far with them. The bright fish had vanished into the depths, and they were entirely alone. It was easy to imagine that there was no dry land left anywhere on earth—that the whole world was covered with endless ocean.

A change seemed to have come over Jesus. His kind face was clouded with anger and shone more brightly than before. Rage burned in his eyes. He appeared to stand taller, and he moved farther away, as if Jonathan, too, were tainted with Adam and Eve's sin and could not be allowed to approach him.

The ocean under Jonathan's feet began to move uneasily. The wind became cold and whipped into a fierce gale, blowing blackened clouds before it that blotted out all the stars and hid the moon in darkness. In seconds, all around him, the once still waters became raging waves, leaping high in the air and crashing down with a deafening roar.

Jonathan was thrown away from Jesus and onto the churning surface of the sea. Terrified, he reached out blindly again for Jesus' hand. But the ocean between them opened suddenly, and from the gaping depths a pillar of water spewed into the air, separating them. It arched so high that Jonathan lost sight of it before it began to fall toward him again. In the distance, he could see another chasm open, then another.

Then the sky, too, burst open, shattered by a sudden bolt of lightning. The clouds were swept away, and Jonathan could see another ocean trembling anxiously in the heavens, waiting for the single word from its master that would call it crashing down upon them.

But Jesus held it back. It hung there, quivering. The storm, too, waited in silence. The web of lightning froze in its place, illuminating the fountains with an eerie crackling light as they paused in midflight at his voiceless command.

Hesitantly, Jonathan lowered his arm from his face and stared at the terrible, frozen hurricane around him.

"I destroyed them," Jesus said finally, in a voice as distant as the thunder. "I destroyed them and all of their wickedness, and along with them I destroyed everything else that I had made. I opened up the windows of heavens, I freed the fountains from deep inside the earth. I let the waters pour down and up and out and over the whole world.

"And everything that moved on the earth died—birds, beasts, men—everything that had the breath of life that *I had given them*—everything died."

Jonathan began to cry then, partly from the frightening tale and the horrible sight, but mostly from the rage he saw in Jesus' eyes and the grief and pain in his voice.

"Couldn't you save anyone?" he sobbed. "Were they *all* evil?"

"On the whole earth," Jesus replied, "there was one man who knew me. His name was Noah."

As he spoke, a dark, box-like form appeared on the distant horizon. It did not look entirely real—more like a dark, quavering shadow—and Jonathan strained his eyes to see what it was.

Jesus pointed toward the shadow. "Before I destroyed the world, I told Noah to build a huge boat called an ark, and I gave him very specific instructions so that it would be strong and safe.

"It took him many years to finish it, and while he worked, he tried to warn these wicked men that I was going to destroy them. He tried to persuade them to stop doing evil things and to come with him and his family on the ark. All they had to do was believe him, and I would save them. They did not have to do anything except believe him, and get on the ark.

"But they only laughed at him."

Jonathan watched as the distant shadow solidified into the shape of an enormous boat, sitting low in the waters, struggling against the winds.

"When the ark was finished, I went through the world and gathered up two of every kind of creature that I had made—I could not bear to destroy all of them. They, at least, still knew me and came when I called to them. So I led them into the ark with Noah and his family.

"Then I closed the door and sealed it myself. And everyone inside was safe for a whole year while I flooded the earth."

He paused. As Jonathan watched, he closed up the sky again, directed the fountains back into their deep wells, then melted the angry waves down into a smooth, cold mirror of water.

Jesus motioned around them to the vast, unbroken, now deathly silent ocean. "It looked like this when I was finished. All of my beautiful creation, destroyed."

Jonathan could not contain his tears as he stared at the endless sea. But as he thought more about it, he nodded to himself. It really did make sense. God could not allow such evil to continue. Surely so much water would wash all the sin out of the world, and then everything would be the way Jesus had intended it to be in the beginning.

He looked hopefully toward the image of the dark boat on the horizon. "Did things get better after that?" he asked, certain that the story was about to come to a quick and happy ending. "Did you wash all the sin out of the world?"

He was very surprised when Jesus answered, "No. Water cannot wash sin out of anyone—certainly not out of the whole world. Sin is a much more horrible thing than you realize. And remember, Noah was a child of Adam and Eve, and he still had that sin in him. So did his family."

"*Noah* had sin?"

"Yes."

"But I don't understand. If he had sin, then why did you save him? If he had sin, didn't he have to die, too?"

"Yes," Jesus answered. "But I saved him from the flood because he found grace in my eyes."

"Grace?" Jonathan frowned. "What's that?"

"Grace," Jesus told him, "is something good that you get but that you do not deserve."

Jonathan was still confused. "Grace," Jesus went on, "is when your mother gives you a piece of chocolate cake when you really deserve to be sent to bed without supper. Grace is when your father gives you a hug and a kiss when you really deserve a spanking. Grace is when you deserve death, and God gives you life instead."

"Oh," Jonathan nodded slowly. "But how can you

do that? You already said that wherever there is sin, there has to be death to pay for it. *Always.*"

"That's right," Jesus said, but he did not explain. Instead, he commanded, "Scoop up a handful of seawater."

Jonathan did.

"Throw it up in the air," Jesus told him.

Jonathan tossed it high above their heads. Just as the droplets began to fall back toward them, the moonbeams caught them in midflight and scattered them in a misty arc across the sky.

Jonathan stared in astonishment. A huge rainbow rose from the sea at his feet. Following the path of mist, it stretched out over the sea toward the pale moon and beyond the distant ark. Its spectrum of red, orange, yellow, green, blue, and purple glowed in the bright moonlight, and the sea reflected its glittering colors in every direction toward the horizon.

"When the waters of the flood went down," Jesus said, "and everyone came out of the ark, I made a promise to Noah—I would never again destroy the earth with water. And so that he would remember my promise, I drew my rainbow across the sky for him to see. And now, whenever you see my rainbow, you can remember my promise, too."

Jonathan knelt suddenly on the sea at the base of the glorious rainbow. "I love you, Jesus," he said softly.

Jesus immediately took him in his arms again. As he did, the tall and distant image of angry, righteous holiness that Jonathan had seen before was gone. Here again was Jonathan's Jesus. Righteous, yes. Holy, yes. But close, loving, forgiving. *His.*

Holding him tightly, Jesus replied, "And I love you, Jonathan—so much! Look!" he said and pointed.

Droplets of water were still falling from the sky. But instead of splashing back into the ocean, they were rearranging into a sparkling picture, a great silver scene made of mist, spread for their eyes beneath the rainbow. From the open doors of the huge boat, Jonathan could see animals of every kind hurrying out, dashing away happily in every direction. A family approached them. Their eyes were bright and thankful, and they reached shimmering hands up toward heaven.

But one man was awed and kneeling, as Jonathan was, at the rainbow's base. There was a pile of stones in front of him. As Jonathan watched, he took a baby lamb, set it on the pile of stones, and to Jonathan's dismay, killed it with a single stroke of his knife. As he bowed his head to pray, the body of the little animal burst into flames and burned to ashes on the stones.

Jonathan was appalled. "Why did he do that?!" he demanded indignantly.

Jesus was solemn. "Even Noah, who loved me very much, was a sinful man," he replied. "And the penalty for sin is death."

"But he didn't die—the lamb did! *It* didn't have sin, did it?"

"No," Jesus replied. "That is why it was able to die in Noah's place. Its blood covered Noah's sin."

Jonathan was not convinced. "You mean Noah didn't have any more sin after that?"

Jesus shook his head. "Oh, no. He still had sin. The waters of the flood could not take sin away, and the blood of an animal cannot take sin away. But it reminded us of the Savior that would come someday who *could* take sin away. Noah knew my Father's promise, and he believed it, so he showed his faith by sacrificing the lamb."

Jonathan sighed heavily. This was very hard to understand.

But Jesus just said reassuringly, "Come. Let's walk some more." And taking his hand again, Jesus led him up the rainbow and across the sky.

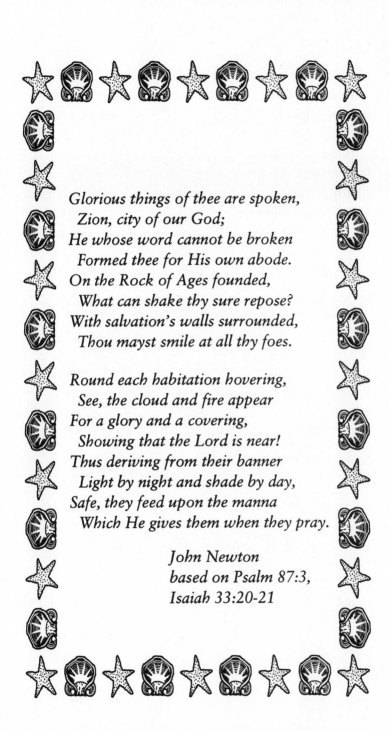

Glorious things of thee are spoken,
  Zion, city of our God;
He whose word cannot be broken
  Formed thee for His own abode.
On the Rock of Ages founded,
  What can shake thy sure repose?
With salvation's walls surrounded,
  Thou mayst smile at all thy foes.

Round each habitation hovering,
  See, the cloud and fire appear
For a glory and a covering,
  Showing that the Lord is near!
Thus deriving from their banner
  Light by night and shade by day,
Safe, they feed upon the manna
  Which He gives them when they pray.

John Newton
based on Psalm 87:3,
Isaiah 33:20-21

5

God's Chosen People

The rainbow rose steeply, and soon the sea was far behind them. On and on they climbed, higher and higher. Soon, they reached the lowest of the scattered clouds. Jonathan could not resist. Giggling, he hopped from the rainbow into one of the wispy cushions, sank down into its softness, and dangled his legs off the side.

He gazed enchanted at the world beneath them. They were so high up! He could barely see the waves below, and he thought (though he was not sure) that he could just make out the beach in the distance. The clouds were especially fascinating as they floated mysteriously past; but strangely, the stars did not seem any closer, even from here.

For a while, he listened to the breathtaking silence, straining to hear a whisper of the sea. But they were far beyond it all, perched on the bright spectrum of God's promise.

"What happened after the flood?" he asked finally, gazing thoughtfully at the rainbow. "Did the sin get worse?"

"Yes," Jesus replied. "Once again, the people multiplied in number. And once again, they became full of sin and refused to obey me. I told them to spread out and fill the whole earth; but instead, they decided that they would build a tall city that stretched all the way up to heaven and live there together."

He gestured around them. "Imagine. They thought that they could build a tower as high as my rainbow, or my clouds, or my heavens."

Jonathan tried, but could not imagine a city as high as these clouds; and the rainbow stretched on above them, high up and out of sight. "They must have been very proud to think so," he said.

"Yes," Jesus said. "Sin makes you proud. But I did not let them finish the city. I made them all speak different languages, so that they could not understand each other, and they had to stop building. *Then* they scattered over all the earth."

"Did they listen to you then?" Jonathan asked, only a little hopefully.

Jesus shook his head. "No. They became more sinful than ever and forgot all about me. They even made statues out of wood and stone, called them gods, and worshiped them instead of me. *That* was the worst sin of all. They belonged to my enemy now— not to me. But I still loved them, and I wanted them back."

Jonathan was becoming impatient with all the sin in this story. "What *for*?" he said indignantly. "If they were so evil, why would you want them?"

"Because I made them," Jesus reminded him gently. "Don't you remember the little girl?"

Jonathan saw what he meant and was instantly ashamed, but Jesus continued. "Wouldn't you want me to go and get her back if my enemy stole her away from me?"

"Yes," Jonathan admitted.

"So that is what I started to do. I chose one nation out of the whole world to be mine. I made these people my own treasured possession—I showed myself to them and gave them my laws to follow. I wanted them to love me and be an example of my goodness to the sinful world that hated me.

"I gave them a beautiful land to live in—a rich land that I loved and cared for myself. As long as they remembered me and kept my law, they lived in that land, and I protected them from all harm.

But when they forgot me and broke my laws, I disciplined them—not to destroy them, but to bring them back to me. And finally, when the time was right, the Savior that my father had promised to Adam and Eve came out of this nation."

"Yes—I want to hear about *him*," Jonathan demanded eagerly. "When did he come? Did he take the sin out of the world? How did he do it?"

"Not quite yet," Jesus said patiently. "First, I will tell you three stories about my people. They will help you understand the Savior better when I tell you about him."

"All right," Jonathan agreed, "but would you tell me about the land you gave them, too? Is it close to where I live?"

"No," Jesus replied, "but I can take you there. Would you like to see it?"

"Oh, yes!" Jonathan hopped to his feet. "How will we get there?"

Jesus looked down at the ocean below and saw that

the moon was just about to sink over the horizon. He took the silver crescent in his hands. Tilted back on its curved edge, it was just the right size and shape for a man and a small boy to step into and sail away into the night.

With a cry of delight, Jonathan bounded into the magical boat. Then, as he watched in awe, Jesus caught a passing cloud, shook it out into a billowing sheet, and set it as a sail over the shining craft. He stepped in next to Jonathan, and directed the wind in toward the horizon.

And when the silver moon set over the sleeping seas, it took with it two passengers toward the promised land.

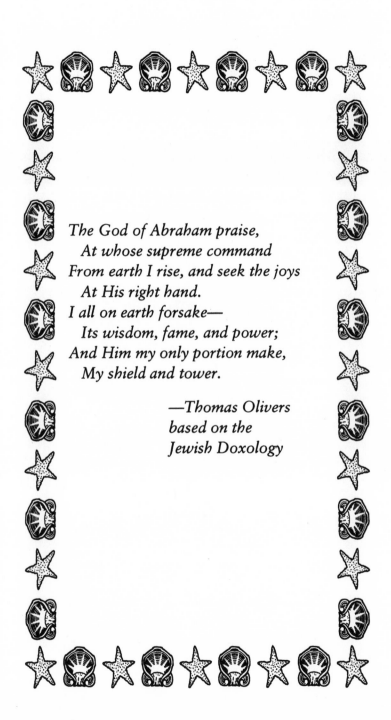

The God of Abraham praise,
    At whose supreme command
From earth I rise, and seek the joys
    At His right hand.
I all on earth forsake—
    Its wisdom, fame, and power;
And Him my only portion make,
    My shield and tower.

—Thomas Olivers
based on the
Jewish Doxology

6

A Father's Greatest Love

As the wind blew them briskly along and the rainbow dissolved into the night behind them, Jesus began to speak again. Jonathan listened in rapt attention as they sat together on the floor of the shining boat.

"I chose a man named Abraham to be the father of my people," Jesus began. "Abraham was my close friend—he loved me very much, and he trusted me. I even came and spoke with him in person from time to time, like I am doing now with you."

Until this moment, it had not occurred to Jonathan that his visit with Jesus was anything unusual. He blinked in surprise. "You mean you don't come to see everybody?"

"No. Only a very few."

Jonathan hesitated. "Well," he ventured at last, "you've come to everyone in *my* family."

Jesus shook his head. "No, not like this. You're the only one."

Jonathan's frown deepened. "But you said that all of them knew you—and that you want *everyone* to know you. If you don't talk to them . . . ?" his voice trailed off helplessly.

"But I *do* talk to them," Jesus reassured him. "I have told them all the stories I am telling you now—and also many, many others—in a book called the Bible. This book tells all about how and why I made the world and the people in it, where the sin came from, and how they can become free from it and be with me again. *Anyone* can know me by reading and believing what I have written in this book or by talking to someone who has read it and wants to share it."

"Oh," Jonathan nodded carefully, then added, "I think I have seen this book."

"You have," Jesus agreed. "There are several in your house—that is how your mommy and daddy and all the rest of your family came to know me. Each time they read it, they learn more and get to know me better and better. And on the first day of every week, they gather at church with others who love me, to learn more from this book, to share with each other, and . . . "

"And to sing!" Jonathan interrupted, leaping to his feet in excitement. "They *sing*! I remember now! I've been there, haven't I? A big place—with lots and lots of people who sing!"

Jesus smiled. "That's right."

"That's my favorite part!" Jonathan told him earnestly. "I mean, the singing. I can't understand any of the words, but the music—I can feel it inside me. Sometimes I wish it would never stop. And I *always* wish I could sing with them, but it's still nice just to hear it. Don't you like it, too?"

"Oh, yes, very much. I love their singing."

"Are they singing for you?" Jonathan wanted to know.

"Yes," Jesus replied.

Jonathan nodded again. "*That* must be why it is so beautiful. I'll try to remember next time I hear it. It will make it even better!"

But suddenly, as he thought more about it, his face fell. "But I can't sing for you," he said sadly, "and I can't read your book. I can't even understand if someone tells me about it." His cheeks flushed, and he turned away, afraid for a moment that he might cry.

"Come here, child," Jesus said gently and drew the little boy down into his lap. Cradling him protectively in his arms, he stroked Jonathan's hair and kissed his face softly. "Don't worry," he said. "I knew when I made you that you would not be able to do these things—I never *intended* you to do them. For you, most things that people do are not even important."

Jonathan put his arms around his friend. "But what about the things that *are* important?" he asked.

Jesus touched Jonathan's chin and tilted his face up until the boy was looking right into his eyes. "I will give you those things," he promised. "I will provide *everything* you need out of my great riches and glory. That is why I came to you tonight."

"To teach me those things?"

"Yes."

Jonathan seemed satisfied with the reply. In fact, he suddenly felt fortunate. After all, what could there be in *any* book, or in *any* song, that could compare to sailing the night sky in the loving arms of the Creator? A great joy welled up inside him, and he snuggled contentedly against Jesus' chest.

Once again, he found himself gazing at the heavens,

flooded with those glimmering lights that so beautifully lit the clouds around them and the ocean below. He remembered that the little girl had said that Jesus called them all by name, but he wondered how that could be. There were so many of them!

"Can you count them?" Jesus' voice startled him out of his musings.

"I don't think so," Jonathan said, thinking, *Where would I even start?*

Jesus continued, "I once promised my friend Abraham that he would have as many children and grandchildren and great-grandchildren as there are stars in the sky and grains of sand on the beach. There would be so many that no one would be able to count them."

Jonathan recalled the miles of sand on the beach where he had played with the seagulls, and as he compared that memory with this vast shining sky, he shook his head in wonder. "How could one man have so many children?" he asked.

"Abraham wondered the same thing," Jesus answered, "because he had no children at all when I made him that promise, and he and his wife Sarah were much too old to have a baby."

"You could make one for him," Jonathan offered helpfully. "I saw you do it!" The image of the lovely little girl still danced in his mind, and he smiled to remember her.

Jesus nodded. "Abraham and Sarah waited many years for me to keep my promise. At last, Sarah had a beautiful baby boy, and they named him Isaac. He was the only child they ever had, and Abraham loved him more than anything in the world."

"I think my daddy loves me that much," Jonathan said confidently.

Now Jesus, too, looked above them at the stars. As he continued with the story, he took a handful of them and began to rearrange them into another shining picture even more beautiful than the one of mist beneath the rainbow.

"Isaac became a handsome young man," he continued, "and Abraham looked forward with great confidence to seeing all those grandchildren and great-grandchildren I had promised that he would have."

The stars in Jesus' hands became a vast landscape of rolling hills. There were tents nearby and large herds of animals of the faraway fields. Jonathan recognized Abraham as he took shape, and the strong young form of Isaac, and his mother Sarah working nearby.

"Then one day," Jesus said in a strange voice, "I said to Abraham, 'Take your son Isaac, whom you love so much, and offer him to me as a burnt sacrifice.'"

Jonathan sat straight up, aghast. "You mean like the little lamb that Noah killed?!" he cried. "But *why?*"

"Abraham wondered why, too," Jesus said, "but he did as I told him. He and Isaac went far away. Abraham built the altar and told Isaac what I had said. He even put his son on the stones and had raised the knife to kill him."

The scene was playing out in the stars above their heads, but Jonathan could hardly bear to look at it.

"How could he do that?" he said in a hoarse whisper. "He loved Isaac so much. How could he kill him?"

Jesus' answer was very soft. "Because he loved me even more. When he lifted his hand to kill his son, I was sure how much he really loved me. I didn't really want him to kill Isaac, and I stopped him just in time. And look!"

Jonathan looked up at the flaming starry altar, the image of the man with tears on his face embracing his beloved son . . . and something else.

"Jesus," he said cautiously. "What is that in the bush next to them? Something is moving."

"Look closer," Jesus told him. Jonathan stood up to get a better look. Jesus steered the craft around the scene so that Jonathan could see behind it. "It's an animal!" he said excitedly. "What is it? How did it get there?"

"It's a ram," Jesus said. "I put it there myself. What do you think they did with it?"

Jonathan's mind raced. The story was vividly familiar. Where had he heard it before? Then he remembered—Noah!

"Did they put it on the altar?" he asked excitedly.

"Yes."

"You mean, instead of Isaac?"

"That's right. The ram took Isaac's place."

"Just like the lamb . . . ," Jonathan frowned, thinking very hard. These stories were very different but somehow the same. Jesus waited patiently, letting Jonathan work things through.

"The ram died instead of Isaac?" Jonathan repeated.

"Yes."

"Did Isaac still have sin?"

"Yes. But again, it reminded my Father of the Savior He promised to send."

Jonathan sat down again and pondered that until the scene was far behind them. Try as he might, he could not understand the connection between these sacrificed animals and the promised Savior.

Finally, the little boy gave up. "I think," he sighed, "that you are going to have to tell me the next story."

I will sing to the Lord,
  For He has triumphed gloriously!
The horse and its rider
  He has thrown into the sea!

The Lord is my strength and song,
  And He has become my salvation;
He is my God, and I will praise Him;
  My father's God, and I will exalt Him.

Song of Miriam
Exodus 15:1-2 NKJV

7

Death Passes Over

The silver boat began to descend through the cloud layers and after a while came to rest on the surface of the sea. As it brushed lightly against the gentle waves, Jesus began his next tale.

"Isaac's son Jacob had twelve sons, and their children and grandchildren became the great nation which I had promised to Abraham. The nation was called Israel.

"For four hundred years, Israel lived in the land of Egypt. After a few generations, there were so many of them that the Egyptians became afraid of them and made them their slaves. Then my people had to work very hard all the time, and the Egyptians were cruel to them.

"When at last it was time to bring Israel out of Egypt and into the land I had promised to Abraham, I chose a man named Moses to lead them there. But Pharaoh, who ruled Egypt, would not let them leave."

Jonathan leaned on the side of the boat and trailed his fingers in the salty waves, but he was still listening intently. When Jesus paused, Jonathan looked up at him, his eyes begging him to continue.

"Now Pharaoh did not know me—he even believed that *he* was a god, and he refused to listen to Moses. So I sent terrible plagues to Egypt to show him that *I* was the God of these people, not him.

"I turned their water into blood. I covered their land with millions of frogs, lice, and flies. I sent a terrible disease to kill all of their animals and another disease that covered the people with awful sores. I sent hailstorms and locusts to kill all their trees and the food they were growing in the fields, and I covered the land with a darkness so thick that the people could not even leave their houses.

"But even after all this, Pharaoh would not let Israel go. So then I sent the tenth, and worst, plague."

What could be worse than all that? Jonathan wondered.

Jesus leaned on the side of the boat next to Jonathan and began to draw another picture, this time on the surface of the sea. As he drew with his finger, the water parted in little channels but did not fill in again. Soon, Jonathan could see a small house drawn in the water. There was an entire family inside—a father, mother, children, grandparents—and they were all in a terrible hurry. The women were standing at the fire hastily cooking a meal. The children were scurrying about, frantically gathering things and setting them together near the door. The men were worried and impatient. Some were outside herding the animals together. Others were standing together and talking in low voices or anxiously urging the children to hurry.

"What are they doing?" Jonathan asked curiously.

"Just what I told them to do—getting ready to leave Egypt," Jesus replied. "'Get dressed,' I said. 'Gather all your family and flocks and possessions together, and prepare your last meal in Egypt.'

"Now this meal was very important, so I told them that they must follow my instructions *exactly*."

He removed his hand from the water, but the figures in his drawing had come to life. As he described the meal, the little Hebrew family hurried to obey him while Jonathan watched.

"Pick out a perfect young male sheep or goat." They did so even as he spoke. "It must be perfect in every way—no spots, no diseases. Kill it at twilight, and put its blood on the top and sides of your front door."

Jonathan stared as the men took the goat they had just killed and hastily splattered its blood on the doorframe. They were in too much of a hurry to be neat, and the blood ran down over the door and some of it spilled onto the step.

Jesus continued. "Then roast the animal in the fire, and eat it in a hurry—standing up, packed and ready to leave. Don't even take the time to let your bread rise. And if there is any meat left over, don't try to keep it—let it burn up in the fire."

Jonathan did not think that the hurried and anxious family enjoyed their meal very much. The adults were nervous, and the children were frightened by their parents' hushed whispers, the upset routine, and not least by the ugly bloodstains on the door. As they finished the meal, they put the scraps on the fire with what was left of the goat's carcass and stood aside, waiting in a hushed silence, as it burned away. All of them seemed relieved that the meal was over.

But then Jesus told them, "This meal will be called

the Passover. You must remember it and celebrate it every year from now on."

Jonathan broke his awed silence. "*Every year?*" he gasped. "What for?"

"So that they would never forget what happened next," Jesus said. Again, his voice began to sound distant and terrible, but this time he rested his hand reassuringly on Jonathan's shoulder as he spoke of the judgment.

"At midnight, I brought the tenth plague into Egypt myself. I went to every house in the entire land and looked to see if there was blood on the door. If there was no blood, I killed the first born in that house. I did not miss anyone—rich families, poor families, animals—even Pharaoh's oldest son died that night. No one escaped this last plague . . . except the Children of Israel. They had obeyed me, and when I saw the blood on their doors, I passed over their houses and did not go in. That is why it was called the *Passover*."

"Oh," Jonathan nodded.

"When I was finished," Jesus continued, "the Egyptians were so frightened and angry that they chased Moses and all my people out of Egypt that very night."

"Where did they go?" Jonathan asked.

"Into the desert," Jesus explained. "But I was there waiting for them, and I guided them myself. During the day, I appeared before them in a pillar of cloud, and at night, I guided them in a bright pillar of fire. I was always there in front of them. They could see me all the time, day or night."

He seemed to be finished now with the picture he had drawn in the water because as he turned away, the scurrying figures suddenly vanished with a faint splash and a hiss of foam as the waves filled them in again.

"But soon," Jesus went on, "Pharaoh became sorry that he had let them go. He gathered up his army and his horses and chariots and went after them to force them back to Egypt. When the Israelites saw them coming, they were camping in the desert next to this sea," he gestured at the water around them, "and there was no place for them to go. The Egyptians were coming from the west, and the Red Sea was stopping them in the east."

"What did you do?" Jonathan wondered.

"Oh, I had planned all this," Jesus reassured him, "but the Israelites were still very frightened. They forgot that I had sent the plagues on Egypt, that I had passed over their houses and spared them from the tenth plague of death, and that I had led them away from Egypt myself in the pillar of cloud and of fire."

This upset Jonathan greatly. "How could they *forget*?!" he cried. "*I* wouldn't forget all *that*!"

"Maybe," Jesus said cautiously. "But they did. They thought I was going to leave them there alone to die in the desert, and they told Moses that they would rather go back to Egypt and be slaves again."

"After all you did to bring them out?!" Jonathan cried indignantly. "How could they? And besides, you were right there in the cloud and the pillar of fire—they could *see* you!"

"All right," Jesus answered and pointed ahead of them. Land had become clearly visible on the horizon. It was barren, dry, and rocky, and not at all inviting.

"When they stood on the shore and watched the Egyptians coming at them," Jesus said, "they did not have any boats. Now, you pretend that you don't have a boat. Get out and run to that land."

Jonathan was surprised at the instruction, but then he shrugged, "Okay," and reached out for Jesus' hand. But Jesus shook his head. "No," he said. "Go by yourself. I'll stay here and watch you."

Jonathan was sure he could not be serious. "By myself?" he repeated. "Without you? I'll fall in the water and drown!"

But Jesus remained firm. "Do what I tell you," he insisted. "Hurry."

Jonathan put his hands on the side of the boat and looked into the dark water. It looked very cold and very deep, and he shuddered as a formless black shadow glided past, far below the surface. The waves seemed suddenly higher now, and the white foam on their crests looked horribly sinister as they rolled past him. He hesitated, started to climb up on the edge of the boat, then instead put his hand in the water to test it. The surface did not even begin to hold him, and his hand came away dripping wet. All his courage left him and he turned and threw himself at Jesus.

"No!" he cried. "I can't!"

"But Jonathan," Jesus said patiently. "I'm right here. You can *see* me."

Jonathan flushed with shame, remembering his own words. But the realization only made him angry, and he stamped his foot and started to cry. "I don't care," he sobbed. "I don't want to! I'm not getting out!"

"But don't you remember how I brought you here? Do you think I would let anything happen to you now?"

"No!" Jonathan sulked, very angry with himself now. "But I can't get out by myself. I'm afraid!"

"So were the Israelites," Jesus explained gently. "They were wrong—and so are you—not to trust me. But I loved them just like I love you, and I fought the Egyptians for them while they watched."

Jonathan was still sulking and embarrassed, so Jesus picked him up and wiped away his angry tears. Gradually Jonathan's curiosity began to replace his embarrassment, and he was sorry he had gotten mad. He wanted to hear the rest of the story, but Jesus waited until he grudgingly whispered, "So what did you do then?"

Jesus continued with the story as if nothing had happened. "I moved behind them until the pillar of cloud stood between them and the armies of Egypt. And then I told Moses to stretch out his staff over the sea."

"Why? What did that do?"

"Look," Jesus pointed to the far shore.

The brisk breeze that had blown over them began to strengthen as he spoke, following his outstretched hand over the water and toward the shore. Stronger and stronger it blew, until a trench began to form in the water under the pressure of the wind. Still the wind blew stronger, and then the water began to move apart.

Jonathan watched, speechless, as the trench became deeper and deeper, and the walls of parted water grew higher and higher above his head. Almost before he could catch his breath, the water parted entirely to reveal the floor of the ocean, and by the time the boat settled down on it, it was completely dry.

"Ooohhh," Jonathan sighed. This was incredible! And this time Jesus did not have to ask him—he bounded out of the boat onto the dry ocean floor and ran out between the wet, towering walls. He gazed in wonder around him, lost in utter astonishment.

"It's wonderful!" the little boy gasped. There was nothing else to say about it. "It's wonderful!" he repeated helplessly.

Jesus, too, had left the boat and was standing beside him again. He laughed. "You have not seen or heard even the *beginning* of wonderful things," he assured him. "But the Israelites were as happy as you are to see this. They simply walked across the sea on dry ground, while the Egyptians were hidden behind my cloud and could not follow them." He took Jonathan's hand again in his own.

"Let's run!" he said playfully. So they ran like the wind between the towering walls of the sea. Jonathan savored every breath of wind that tousled his hair, the sensation of the dry sand under his every step, the wonderful salty taste of the air. He ran faster and faster—not even Matthew and Mark could catch him today! He felt as though he could run forever, but all too soon they reached the other side, and he collapsed weary but happy onto the far shore and looked back out to the oceanic canyon they had just crossed.

But although they were clear of it, it was not empty! He stood up again and pointed back in alarm. "Who is *that*?" he demanded.

Emerging into the dry passage came an army of men—some on horseback and some in horse-drawn chariots. Jonathan was not sure they were real—they looked more like rippling, living statues molded of seawater—but there were thousands of them, charging directly at them, waving swords and shouting angry threats.

Jesus explained. "Pharaoh's army followed my people into the sea," he said, "and I watched them from the pillar of fire and cloud. When all of them were on the floor of the sea between the walls of water . . . ," his voice trailed off.

"What?!" Jonathan demanded, tearing his gaze away from the approaching army. The horses were at a full gallop and would soon reach them. He could hear the thundering hooves and see their angry eyes. "*What happened then?!*"

"Jonathan," Jesus told him, "stretch out your hand over the water."

Jonathan obeyed. Instantly, the tops of the walls of water began to curl inward, so slowly that Jonathan wanted to scream at them, "Hurry! *Hurry!*" Their fall from their great height down onto the animated Egyptian army seemed to take hours. But they finally crashed against the bottom, and the huge hole in the sea was filled in an instant. A gigantic fountain briefly marked the place where the canyon had been, but it, too, crashed back with incredible force. When the waves finally settled, they were alone on the shore again.

"That," Jesus said, "was the end of Pharaoh and his entire army—all his chariots and horsemen. Not one of them survived. And when the Israelites saw them lying dead on the shore, *then* they believed me."

Jonathan could not take it all in at once but just stood there with his mouth gaping open. There was not a trace of the path they had taken. Nothing but water. The crescent moon, its sail scattered by the desert wind, was beginning to sink slowly in the west. And, here he was, too—safe on the shore. Safe with Jesus.

He gazed at his friend with new wonder. The entire beach was bathed in the light of the man's face—even his clothes gleamed with their own white glow in the darkness. Jonathan suddenly remembered their talk on Grandma's farm.

"Jesus, are you God?" he had asked.

"Yes," Jesus had replied.

Overwhelmed and trembling with awe, Jonathan knelt again, as he had done at the rainbow, not even willing to meet Jesus' eyes. "I won't *ever* doubt you again," he promised in a breathless whisper. "Not *ever!*"

Great is Thy faithfulness,
  O God my Father—
There is no shadow
  of turning with Thee.
Thou changest not,
  Thy compassions they fail not;
As Thou hast been,
  Thou forever wilt be.

Great is Thy faithfulness!
  Great is Thy faithfulness!
Morning by morning
  new mercies I see!
All I have needed
  Thy hand hath provided—
Great is Thy faithfulness,
  Lord, unto me!

Thomas O. Chisholm

8

Mountains of Thunder and a Healing Serpent

The beach where they were standing was bleak and rocky, and Jonathan was not at all looking forward to walking very far in this place. But while he was gazing distastefully at the unfriendly surroundings, Jesus was very busy with something at the edge of the water. Jonathan approached him curiously.

"What are you doing?" he asked.

Jesus did not answer or glance up at him but continued working quickly, gathering up great handfuls of wet sand frosted with seafoam. Even before Jonathan could repeat the question, the pile of sand began to take shape. As he watched, Jesus carved away an enormous head and neck, then sculpted four powerful legs, solidly balanced on massive hooves. He brushed his hand across the figure's back, and the wind swept the loosened sand into a long, flowing tail. Within seconds, the largest, most incredible stallion Jonathan could ever imagine stood on the shore beside him, lifelike in every respect except that it was made of wet sand and stood statue-still.

Jonathan gasped, gazing in wonder. The horse seemed to look directly at him. Its eyes were wide and its nostrils flaring; its strong muscles looked tensed and ready to leap into battle, and its elegant mane and tail flowed behind it like banners in the wind.

Jesus seemed quite satisfied with his work. "I have given the horse its strength," he quoted softly to himself, "and clothed his neck with thunder . . . His majestic snorting strikes terror. He paws in the valley, and rejoices in his strength; he gallops into the clash of arms, and mocks at fear, and is not frightened . . . "

Jonathan approached it hesitantly. This particular horse was *not* snorting or pawing at the moment, so he stroked its neck gently. His hand came away coated with wet sand, but his touch left no fingerprints on the horse's perfectly formed features.

"It's just made of sand," he murmured. "What holds it together?"

"I do," Jesus replied matter-of-factly, dusting off his hands. "Everything in all of creation is held together by me."

Then he seemed to forget all about the statue. "Let's walk a little bit this way," he said to Jonathan and started slowly off along the shore.

Jonathan could hardly bear to tear his gaze from the incredible stallion, but when he realized that he might be left behind, he hurried after his friend. As soon as he caught up, Jesus resumed the story where he had left off.

"After I led my people out of Egypt," he said, "I showed them many other wonderful things—great things that had never happened since the day I created man on the earth.

"I chose these people for myself because I loved Abraham, and Isaac, and Jacob. I took their nation out of Egypt. I tested them. I disciplined them. I performed many awesome miracles, right in front of their eyes. I spoke to them myself in my own voice out of the pillar of fire and gave them my own laws. I fought for them in their wars and defeated other nations that were much greater than they were.

"With my own strength, I led them to the land I had promised Abraham. All this—so that they would know me. They would know that *I am God*. I am in heaven above, and on the earth below. There is no other.

"All they had to do in return was obey me, and everything would go well with them and their children, and they would live for a long time in the good land that I had given to them. It would be theirs forever."

"Did they do it?" Jonathan asked.

Jesus' reply was edged with weariness. "From the very beginning, right after leaving Egypt, these people would not trust me," He said. "Only three days after I destroyed the Egyptian army—right in front of their eyes—they forgot about it. They were in the desert, you see, with no water. And when they found some water, it was too bitter to drink. Instead of trusting me to provide for them, they complained to Moses that they would have been better off if they had stayed in Egypt. So I turned the bitter water into good water so they could drink it.

"But later, they began to get hungry, and again they forgot that I had promised to take care of them. Again they complained to Moses and said that I had led them out of Egypt to starve them to death in the desert.

"So I fed them, and not with just *any* food. I covered the desert ground with quail every evening, and each morning sent them a sweet, white bread from heaven itself. There was plenty for everyone, and on the sixth day of the week, I gave them enough for two days so that they could rest on the seventh. I fed them every day for many years—the entire time they were in the desert.

"But the next time they were in a place where there was no water, they forgot that I had given them water before. Again, they complained to Moses, 'We would have been better off in Egypt!' So I brought water out of a dry rock—enough for all of them. But again they forgot, and they grumbled constantly."

Jonathan did not know what to say. He thought about asking Jesus why in the world he had chosen such a *stubborn* nation of people but decided against it. He was beginning to suspect that he really was not any better himself.

Then Jesus turned and looked back to the place where the sand stallion stood waiting. Jonathan followed his gaze and perked up immediately. This Creator simply could not stay idle for long, it seemed.

Jesus laughed, catching the keen sparkle of anticipation in the boy's eyes. "What are you looking at?"

Jonathan was being teased, and he knew it. He smiled broadly. "Do it!" he urged.

"What?" Jesus replied innocently. "From *here*?"

Jonathan rolled his eyes and gave him an impatient look. Jesus laughed, stretched out his hand toward the statue he had made, and as he had done with the little girl, breathed life into it.

The rough sandy texture of the sand statue melted into a shining, silky white as the breath of life touched it from the distance. Instantly, the stallion whirled on its great legs and charged.

Jonathan stumbled backwards, alarmed at the sudden wildness that had appeared in the beast's eyes and the haste at which it thundered toward them. Its pounding hooves hurled torn chunks of sand in every direction. He stared—certain that he would be run over but too stunned to flee—as the great horse halted abruptly only inches away and reared up, almost dancing on its hind legs, and neighing a shrill, joyous response to its new life.

But as he stared in astonishment, Jesus calmly took the wild beast's face in his hands and stroked it with affection. Like the little girl, and the gulls, and the fish under the sea, this great creature obviously knew its creator. Trembling with anticipation, it eagerly awaited its master's instructions.

Jesus turned and beckoned reassuringly to Jonathan, and the boy hesitantly approached the enormous animal. With a pounding heart, and with his eyes tightly clenched shut, he allowed himself to be lifted up onto the horse's broad back. Instantly, Jesus was up behind him, and as Jonathan buried his hands in the glossy mane, they sprang across the desert on the wings of the wind.

And what a wild, magnificent journey it was! The horse's gait was as smooth as if his hooves never touched the ground, and he galloped at such speeds that the wind almost snatched the breath right out of the little boy. Jonathan kept glancing down, half expecting to find himself high in the clouds again, sailing over the desert instead of across it. But no, they were soaring across the barren earth itself at whirlwind speeds, and Jesus' reassuring arms were holding him safely in place. So he leaned low over the stallion's neck, held on with whitened knuckles, and let the overwhelming joy and excitement of the incredible ride fill him to overflowing.

As far as Jonathan was concerned, they could ride like this forever, leaving earth and home far behind without a single regret. But after about an hour, Jesus spoke to the horse, and it cantered to an abrupt halt at the foot of a rugged, barren mountain.

The beast shook its head and snorted impatiently, tossing sand into the wind and stamping, impatient to be off again. But Jesus dismounted and, to Jonathan's intense disappointment, helped him down, too.

"So soon!" Jonathan complained.

"Do you like this creature of mine?" Jesus asked him.

"Oh, yes!" Jonathan sighed. "I could have ridden on and on and on!"

"Then I shall keep him for you," Jesus replied. "And when the armies of heaven, all clothed in clean white linen, follow me into my kingdom on white horses, you may ride him again."

Then he called to the whirlwind, and the stallion galloped away like fire into the heavens.

Jonathan watched wistfully until the creature disappeared. "But I have more to tell you," Jesus said, and Jonathan reluctantly tore his gaze away from the now empty sky.

Jesus turned Jonathan toward the mountain. "It was here that I showed my people even greater things than they had seen before. That mountain," he explained, "is called Sinai. This is where I gave my people my laws. I came down myself in a thick cloud over the mountain in the sight of all the people. Mount Sinai was covered with billowing smoke and thunder and lightning, and the whole mountain shook.

"Then the people heard a loud trumpet blast, and Moses led them out of the camp to meet with me at the foot of the mountain. And when he spoke to me, I answered him.

"But the people were terrified. They would not come near the mountain, and they were afraid for me to speak to them."

"Well, I would have been afraid, too," Jonathan said, "if you had come to my room tonight with thunder and lightning and smoke and trumpets. Why did you do it that way? Why didn't you just talk to them like you are talking to me?"

"I wanted them to know me in all of my power and glory," Jesus explained. "The better they knew me, the easier it would be for them not to sin and to become the righteous and holy nation I wanted them to be.

"But they would not have it. So Moses went up on the mountain by himself, and I gave my laws to him to give to the people."

"What did the laws say?" Jonathan asked.

"There were many of them," Jesus replied. "Most told them how to live a life that would please and honor me. I also told them how to make a tabernacle—a special place where I would live among them.

I would stay in the center of it, behind a thick veil, in a place called the Holy of Holies. No one except the High Priest could ever come in there, and only then under very special rules."

"Why not?" Jonathan asked.

"Because I had been separated from them ever since Adam first sinned in the garden," he explained. "Sin cannot come into the presence of God, remember? So I was separated from them, even while living there with them.

"The tabernacle was also the place where they were to make the sacrifices for their sins, and I gave them laws about how to do that, too."

"More sacrifices?" Jonathan asked. "Like Noah's lamb, and Isaac's ram, and the goat at the Passover?"

"Yes," Jesus replied.

Jonathan shuddered. "They had to keep *doing* that?" he said.

"As long as they sinned, yes," Jesus replied. "And they were full of sin, all the time. They were *born* with it."

"There certainly is a lot of blood in this story," Jonathan grumbled.

Jesus was quick with his reply. "Without the shedding of blood," he said firmly, "there can be no forgiveness for sin. Remember? The penalty for sin is death. So they had to make the sacrifices.

"But even these were not the most important laws. The most important were these two: love the Lord your God with all you heart, soul, and mind; and love each other as much as you love yourself."

"Did they keep all the laws?" Jonathan asked.

"No. In fact, they broke some of them before Moses

ever came back from the mountain. He was away for forty days, and they did not know what had happened to him. When he finally did come down, he found that the people had made a golden calf and were worshiping it instead of me.

"I was very angry and wanted to destroy all of them, like I destroyed the sinful men in the flood. But Moses begged me not to, and I listened to him.

"Over and over I instructed my people, and over and over they disobeyed me. But the worst sin of all was when they arrived at the land I had promised. I told them to go in and take it. I promised that I would destroy all their enemies in front of them and give them the entire land for their own. It was the same promise that I had been giving them for hundreds of years, and I was ready to fulfill it! But when they saw that giants lived in the land, they were afraid and would not go in.

"I was furious! How long would these people refuse to believe in me, in spite of everything I had done for them? Again, I wanted to destroy all of them. But again, Moses begged me to love them and forgive their sin instead, just as I had done ever since they left Egypt.

"So I did forgive them, as he asked." Jesus' voice was hard. "But not one of the men who saw my glory and the miraculous signs and then disobeyed me—not one of them ever saw the land I promised them—not even Moses. Only two out of all those people had trusted me. I let them enter the land, but none of the others."

"What happened to them?" Jonathan asked.

"I left them in the desert for forty years," Jesus

replied, "and let them suffer for their sins until they had all died, and their children were all grown. And *all that time*, they complained and would not trust me.

"Finally, when they said to Moses, 'Why have you brought us up out of Egypt to die in the desert? There is no bread! There is no water! And we hate this miserable food!' I became so angry that I sent a plague of poisonous snakes into their camp.

"The snakes bit them, and many of the people died. At last they realized that they had sinned, and they begged Moses to ask me to take away the snakes. When he did, I listened to him.

"I told him to make a serpent out of bronze and to put it high up on a pole where everyone could see it. Anyone who was bitten by a snake would not die *if* he looked up at the bronze serpent."

"Did Moses do it?" Jonathan asked.

"Yes," Jesus replied. "And many people were still bitten by the snakes. Those who believed me remembered to look at the bronze serpent. They lived. But those who would *not* look at the bronze serpent died."

Jonathan did not know what to say to all this. Why would anyone *not* believe God? And if you had been bitten by the snake, what did you have to lose, anyway? You would be dying!

"I don't get it," he said. "Why didn't they learn to obey you? How could they *be* that way?"

Jesus looked at him. "I told you before," he answered. "Sin is a very terrible thing. These people—*all* the people on the earth—had become slaves to it. They could not escape it on their own. They needed a Savior to take it away."

"Yes!" Jonathan cried. "That's it! You keep mentioning him. When did he come?"

"My Father sent him," Jesus said carefully, "many years later. You see, my people finally did enter the land—I gave it to them as I had promised. And I lived there with them in a temple they built for me, in the Holy of Holies, as I had in the tabernacle in the desert. But they continued to disobey me, over and over again.

"These were *my* people—*I* had chosen them, *my* hand had brought them out of Egypt—and I intended to rule over them and protect them myself. But they insisted on having a king like all the other nations, and most of their kings were wicked and hated me. The people would not keep my laws, and they worshiped these 'gods' they had made of wood and stone.

"So I sent prophets to warn them. 'Turn away from your sins,' they told Israel repeatedly, 'obey the Lord or He will destroy you!'

"Sometimes my people listened and came back to me, but most often, they did not. And as the years went by, their sins became worse and worse, until they became so evil that they even worshiped false gods *in the temple,* in my very presence!

"Finally, I left the Holy of Holies where I had lived among them for so many years. I allowed the evil nations around them to come into the land and to carry the people away to become slaves, like they had been in Egypt. Most of them never came back. But I saved a few for myself, and after many years, I let them return to the land to start over.

"But Jonathan, they were still prisoners of their sin. And they would be forever, without help. I knew that they could never conquer it themselves—no ocean could wash it away, no sacrifice they could make would ever cover it completely.

"So at last, my Father sent me to them. I came to them myself—I became a man, only *without* sin. I lived in the land among them, face to face. I taught them great things and showed them many wonderful miracles so that they would recognize me and believe me when I told them who I was. And finally, I would conquer their greatest enemy—their sin—as I had conquered all the others.

"It was time."

O sacred Head, now wounded,
  With grief and shame weighed down;
Now scornfully surrounded
  With thorns Thine only crown.
How pale Thou art with anguish,
  With sore abuse and scorn—
How does that visage languish
  Which once was bright as morn!

Paul Gerhardt
based on a
Medieval Latin poem
ascribed to
Bernard of Clairvaux

9

The Dead Hill with Empty Eyes

Jonathan remained hushed as Jesus continued speaking. The anguish in Jesus' voice had left his own cheeks streaked with tears, and he believed he could feel in the tightness of his own throat the almost unendurable yearning this Creator held for his people, his despair at the depths of the sin that separated him from them, and his unflinching determination to defeat the enemy that had stolen them and to recover them for himself.

In a tone that was low and still and full of foreboding, Jesus began to describe a city called Jerusalem. As he spoke, his words came alive and painted a living, moving landscape around them. The rocks and the mountain of Sinai faded as dusty, narrow streets appeared beneath Jonathan's feet and stretched into the distance around unseen corners. Walls and doorways grew out of the sand, then solidified into buildings of stone and dried mud. The desert night sounds faded and were replaced by voices of many people and the bustling sounds of midday.

Suddenly, people seemed to be everywhere. Some were carrying baskets of food, several led donkeys, others held children by the hand. All seemed busy about their daily work and took no notice of them. And as Jesus finished speaking, a blue sky swept across the stars, its brightness obliterating the night and replacing it with a clear spring day. It was late morning.

But in spite of the sudden glare, Jonathan was consumed with apprehension as, in the distance, he could hear the ugly growing uproar of an angry mob.

"Jesus, what's going on?" he asked, disoriented and a little frightened.

This time, though, there was no answer. He turned to repeat his question. "Jesus, what . . . "

But Jesus was not there. Jonathan was standing alone on the strange dusty street, two thousand years before his own birth, in the city of old Jerusalem.

⊕

Jonathan wandered for several minutes in growing panic. *Where was he? Why had Jesus left him? What was he was supposed to see here?*

He had no idea which way he should go, and the crowd was growing rapidly. Angry voices clamored in the street, and as they grew closer, he could also hear the despairing cries of mourning women. He was desperately trying to get out of the way when the mob suddenly swarmed around the corner. But the street was too narrow and the crowd too thick, and they were upon him instantly.

Jonathan's panic gave way to terror. He was completely surrounded by the masses and utterly at their mercy. He was too small to see anything through the crowd. The noise was deafening, and he could neither stand still, nor turn around, nor get away. Helplessly, he was swept along the narrow streets with no hope but to somehow keep up with them. More than once he was nearly shoved to the ground. Finally, in a frantic attempt to not be crushed underfoot, he clutched at the robes of a woman ahead of him.

She glanced back dully. She seemed very tall, and her dark eyes and long black hair could have been beautiful. But she was gasping and stumbling, mad with grief, and her eyes were swollen and red, as if she had been weeping for hours. Although she instinctively reached out a hand to steady him, Jonathan did not think she had really seen him.

But her sobs and the echoing broken cries scattered throughout the angry crowd haunted him. *What could be the matter?* he wondered. *What horrible thing is going on?*

By now the mob had driven them down the winding street, far from where Jesus had left him. Jonathan had long ago lost all sense of direction. Vaguely, he realized that they were passing through a huge stone gate and leaving the city streets behind and below them.

The crowd began to spread out then, so Jonathan strained to see what was going on ahead. A low, barren hill rose up ahead of them. Only the ugliest of plants were growing there, and for one terrifying second, Jonathan was sure that he could see the fleshless face of a skull leering at him out of the hillside. Several men worked angrily on its peak with hammers and nails and huge posts of roughly sawn wood that stood upright in the ground.

He was nearer to the front of the crowd now and

could tell that the onlookers were shouting at some-one. He could not guess why or see who it was, but through the crowd he caught an occasional glimpse of a soldier's hand. It was rising and falling with untiring hatred, relentlessly clenching a heavy club. Another hand wielded a bloodied whip that was studded with sharp pieces of bone.

Jonathan recoiled in revulsion and shock. He had never seen anything like this in his life. The fury of the mob and the ugly, staring hill had filled him with an unnamed dread. Now at the sight of this sickening cruelty, his only thought was to run as far away as he could from this hideous place.

At that instant, there was a break in the crowd, and he had a clear view of the soldiers. They were driving a man toward that awful hill, beating him unmerci-fully at every step. Jonathan could not see his face because he was bent almost to the ground under the weight of a huge wooden beam. His back and arms and head were soaked with blood, and he was having difficulty standing. But still the whip and the club fell relentlessly, until at last he stumbled and fell to the ground.

The enraged soldiers shouted louder, but the man was so weak now that no number of kicks or blows could force him to his feet again. Finally realizing that it was hopeless, one of the soldiers scanned the crowd and seized the first strong young man he could reach. Motioning to the wooden beam, he ordered him to pick it up and carry it.

The instant that the soldier's attention turned from the bleeding man, the woman at Jonathan's side dashed forward. Before the other soldiers could shove her away, she collapsed in a heap before the prisoner, sobbing brokenly and clinging to him.

The man looked up and spoke a few words to her that Jonathan could not hear over the roar. His face was bruised and swollen and bloody beyond recognition. But Jonathan could see that someone had twisted a sort of crown out of long, sharp thorns and had pushed it cruelly down into his forehead.

His forehead? A horrible suspicion began to grow in Jonathan's mind. *His forehead?* Then he shook his head decisively. It simply could not be—it was not possible.

But just before the soldiers kicked the woman away from the prisoner, he clutched her arm. "Mary," he said and pointed . . . directly at Jonathan.

Their eyes met for the briefest second. The man was Jesus.

Stunned, Jonathan let the crowd close around him again as they started back toward the hill. He was still rooted to the spot when Mary somehow found him. Still sobbing, she took Jonathan in her arms and carried him with her to the top of the hill.

⊕

The rest of the day passed in numb horror for Jonathan. He could not comprehend what was happening. What was the matter with these people?! Didn't they know? This was *Jesus* they had whipped. This was *Jesus* they had beaten. Jesus who had made them—Jesus who was *God*.

But the ordeal had only begun. When they got to the top of the hill, the soldiers tied his arms to the heavy beam he had been too weak to carry, then nailed his hands to it with huge ugly spikes. Jonathan buried his head in Mary's robe, unable to watch. But even though she held him tightly against her, pressing one ear against her chest and covering the other with her hands, she could not block out the ghastly sounds.

When Jonathan found the courage to look again, they had hoisted the beam up onto one of the tall, upright posts he had seen earlier and fastened it in place. This time, they drove the huge nail through his feet.

And still the people shouted. Still they spit at him and threw things. Someone even tried to give him sour wine to drink. Two other men were nailed to crosses on both sides of him, and even one of *them* was laughing at him.

And he let them do it! Jonathan was dumbfounded.

The clear sky quickly clouded. It grew darker and darker, until it felt like a starless night.

And what reason did the stars have to shine now? Jonathan wondered miserably. Their perfect Creator was dying at the hands of these sinful men.

Jonathan could not bear to watch as the sneers and ridicules continued, and thankfully, he was too far away to hear anything very clearly. From time to time, he thought he could hear Jesus' voice, and once, the crowd became very excited about something he had cried out loudly. But the words had been meaningless to Jonathan.

In the middle of all this madness, the musical voice of the exquisite little girl floated back to him. Jonathan thought of the rainbow, the power of the flood, and the miracle at the Red Sea. As he remembered, he could almost feel the wind that had sailed the crescent moon and the powerful, rippling muscles of that incredible stallion as he sat astride its back, carefully protected by Jesus' arms.

Surely, these people could not possibly understand what they were doing!

Hours and hours went by. Mary stood at a distance, very still and quiet now. She continued to hold Jonathan, often pressing him against her, covering his eyes with her hand, then trying to hide her own face against him. It seemed a long time later when Jesus finally cried out, in a voice that was surprisingly strong—that somehow combined sorrow, fatigue, and triumph, "It is finished!"

Then he died.

Mary sank to her knees, her entire body shuddering with deep, racking sobs. Then it was not only Mary but the whole hill—the whole earth that was shaking. A deafening rumble thundered in Jonathan's ears, and as he watched, a huge boulder near them split into three pieces.

The other onlookers panicked, scattering hysterically in every direction. The air was filled with their frightened cries. But Jonathan was so crushed with grief that he hardly even noticed the earthquake.

What had happened to the awesome power that had created the universe? Where was the mighty hand that had called down the floods of heaven and that had parted the waters of the Red Sea? Where was the great pillar of cloud and fire and those endless legions of angels, all at the command of this mighty Jesus?

Why had he died?

Chaos still surrounded them, but Jonathan and Mary remained still and uncaring. Mary's arms fell limply to her sides. Her head was bowed, and her shoulders shook, but now she made no sound at all. Jonathan touched her hand, then her cheek, but she did not feel it, and he had no idea what else to do. So when the earth finally quieted, he climbed off her lap, hesitated, then slowly began to walk away.

No one took any notice as the little boy passed the weeping women. The crowd of mockers was now strangely subdued by the earthquake, and no one said anything to him. No one shouted at him as he passed the guard of soldiers and one of the dying thieves. No one tried to stop him as he approached the cross and quietly stopped at its foot. No one pushed him away, so he stood there alone, silently and still, staring miserably upwards in anguish and disbelief.

It is finished, Jesus had said.

What could it mean?

What could it mean . . . But Jonathan's mind was dull, as if his head were stuffed with dust, and he could not work anything out. Nothing made sense now, nothing seemed important—not the glories of creation, not the power of God, not the promises of a friend . . .

He did not know how long he stood there, his eyes fixed on the unthinkable. It seemed as though time had stopped and left him there.

But by and by, the soldiers became impatient that the two other men still lived; so they took their clubs, and brutally broke the legs of both of them. One of the soldiers came to Jesus next, and Jonathan did not think he could bear it if they broke his legs, too. But when the soldier saw that he was already dead, he took his spear instead and thrust it into Jesus' side.

Jonathan was vaguely aware that some of the blood and water flowing from the wound had splashed on him, staining his clothes. And on either side of him, the two thieves could no longer hold themselves up to breathe and were dying quickly now, choking horribly.

But Jonathan no longer felt as though he were really standing there, so none of it bothered him very much. He was still staring in a daze when he felt a soft hand on his arm, and Mary led him away.

The crowd had thinned now, but Mary and several other women stubbornly remained at a distance until a man took the body of Jesus down from the cross and wrapped it in a sheet. Then they followed him to a nearby garden and watched carefully as he put the body into an empty tomb and rolled a heavy stone in front of the door.

The women spoke together in low, sorrowful voices for a while, then finally went to their homes. It was nearly nightfall.

⊕

Mary took Jonathan home with her. She gave him a little bread, but he could not eat it, and she herself would touch nothing. So she put him down on a little mat to sleep, then neither looked up nor spoke to him again for the rest of the night.

But he was so haunted with the memories of the day that he could not close his eyes. He watched Mary as she gathered up several jars and set them together by the door. Then she put her head down and cried again.

Jonathan could still hear her sobbing when he finally fell asleep.

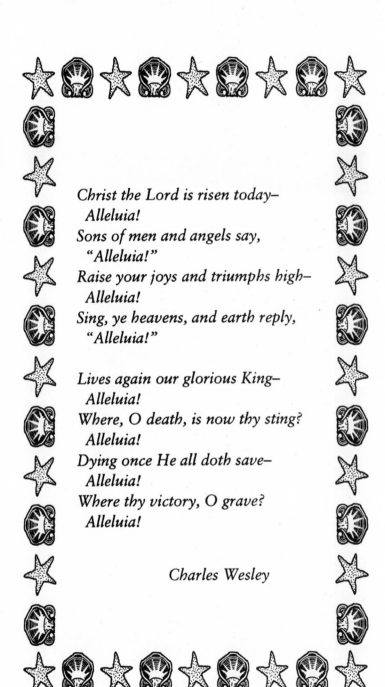

Christ the Lord is risen today–
  Alleluia!
Sons of men and angels say,
  "Alleluia!"
Raise your joys and triumphs high–
  Alleluia!
Sing, ye heavens, and earth reply,
  "Alleluia!"

Lives again our glorious King–
  Alleluia!
Where, O death, is now thy sting?
  Alleluia!
Dying once He all doth save–
  Alleluia!
Where thy victory, O grave?
  Alleluia!

Charles Wesley

10

The Savior

The next morning passed in dull uneventfulness. Still Mary would not eat, and Jonathan sat by himself, thinking. But the only thought he could form clearly was: *Why?*

And he had no answer.

Why had Jesus died? Death was punishment for sin, but Jesus had not sinned. Jesus *could* not sin.

He could think of no explanation.

Why had he let them do it? Surely his angels would have come if he had called them. Those soldiers could never have stood against their flaming swords.

Why hadn't he called them?

No answer came, no matter how hard he tried to think.

The miserable day plodded tediously by. It was hot, despite the low clouds that kept everything so dark and dreary. Mary had long since stopped crying. She simply sat on the floor in a corner, staring at the empty air. Once when Jonathan looked at her, it seemed that she had not moved or even blinked for a very long time. For a single, terrifying instant, he imagined that she might have died, too.

But at last she felt his anxious gaze on her and looked dully toward him. Not knowing what else to do, he crawled across the floor and into her lap. Awkwardly, she put her arms around him, but neither of them felt comforted.

For the first time since he had walked into the night with Jesus, Jonathan thought longingly of home. It seemed so very far away, and he desperately wished to be back there again. He wanted to feel the reassuring touch of his mother, listen to the comforting voices of his sisters and brothers and to his daddy's laughter. He wanted to hear the familiar sounds of dishes clattering in the sink while the telephone rang and Kim held him at the piano. He wanted her to bang on those keys so hard and so loud and so long that he would not be able to think about or even recall what he had seen.

He wanted someone—*anyone*—to sing to him.

But no one was singing today. Jonathan was relieved when the sun finally sank below the houses and darkness settled over the city. He lay down again, but he was so dizzy from trying to make sense out of the senseless that again he could not sleep.

Why Jesus? He was God. He made everything.

He made Adam and Eve, but then they sinned.

And they died because of it.

And their children sinned, and they died. And their children's children sinned, and they died. Every person who was born sinned and died for it.

There certainly is a lot of death in this story, he thought.

Jesus' words rushed back to him. *Death is the*

penalty for sin, his friend had said. *Always, when there is sin, there has to be death to pay for it.*

But then Jesus died, too. And he didn't *have* any sin.

Jonathan closed his eyes, trying to block out the memory. But the barren hill with its mocking, empty eyes and its bloody cross still danced vividly in his mind and seemed to become even clearer as he pressed his hands hard over his eyes to hide it.

The soldiers' harsh laughs tormented him. They became louder and louder, echoing cruelly in his ears even as the night became hushed.

Outside, he could hear thunder rolling in the distance. As it came nearer, black storm clouds let loose a torrent of rain.

Jonathan whimpered softly in his sleep, but no one came to wake him.

Bright lightning ripped the sky open, and Jonathan watched in terror as the waters of heaven hung menacingly above him. This time there was no one to hold them back, and he shrieked as they began to fall. The ground, too, yawned open, and the deep fountains within the earth leaped up to meet the deluge from heaven.

What was it Jesus had said?

A familiar voice came to his dream. *All they had to do was believe what Noah said, and I would save them. They did not have to do anything except believe him and get on the ark.*

A huge wave was surging toward him. "Not me!" Jonathan cried out. "I would have believed him!" Immediately a strong hand grabbed his arm, pulling him against the tide and out of the water.

He could hear Jesus' voice speaking to him over the

raging tempest. *I saved him from the flood because he found grace in my eyes.*

What is grace?

Grace is something good that you get, but that you do not deserve . . . Grace is when God gives you life when you really deserve death.

Then his feet were touching the ground again. He was standing beside a very old, bearded man who was kneeling at a rough stone altar. The flood was gone, and a rainbow stretched across a bright blue sky.

Again, he watched as Noah cut open the lamb's throat. It did not make a sound as its blood poured out over the pile of stones and was consumed with flames.

The smoke scorched his eyes, and the fire gave out a distasteful stench. He turned away, but a familiar voice encouraged him to watch.

That little lamb, it reminded him, *died in Noah's place. Its blood covered Noah's sin.*

But when he looked again, it was not a little lamb, but a ram that was burning there. A man was embracing a handsome young man—his only son, whom he loved so much, who had just been saved from death.

I put it there myself, Jesus' voice said to him. *The ram took Isaac's place.*

Jonathan stretched out a timid finger to touch the alter. It came away sticky with the ram's blood, and he turned in disgust to wipe it on the frame of a nearby doorway. The blood ran down the sides of the doorframe, and more blood streamed down the door from overhead.

There certainly is a lot of blood in this story, he had complained to Jesus.

But without the shedding of blood, the voice replied, *there can be no forgiveness of sin.*

A shriek tore at his heart. Behind him, an Egyptian woman ran madly into the street, clutching the still body of a toddler. Cries of grief were rising in the distance. Then Jonathan saw a tall shining figure, robed in white, and carrying death and judgment in his hands. His familiar righteous face burned with anger, but when he looked toward Jonathan, he saw the blood on the doorway. His expression softened, and he passed by.

Then Jonathan was again swept away by the panic-stricken crowd, only this time into the desert. He could hear the thunder of horses' hooves behind him in the distance, and they were all filled with dread. *We must run faster . . .*

They came up short against a vast sea.

The shining figure became a billowing cloud, stretching from the sand high up into the sky, and flooded the desolate landscape with light. It called a heavy wind from across the sea, which came instantly and parted the water into two towering walls, exposing a dry path between them. Jonathan fled out onto the sea floor, praying that the wind would hold back the towering sea until he had crossed safely.

Suddenly, he cried aloud and fell hard against the sand, his foot stinging painfully. The ground around him was writhing with snakes. Another bit him on the arm, and as he desperately tried to crawl away, he felt a third sharp sting on his hand.

I'm going to die, he thought.

Death is the penalty for sin, his friend's voice reminded him sadly. *Sin cannot come into the presence of the perfect God. Any creature who sins must be separated from me forever. That is what death is.*

Suddenly, the unthinkable realization struck Jonathan with a bite more deadly than those of the fiery serpents.

He had listened carefully to Jesus' story. He had grieved for Adam, admired Noah, and marveled at Abraham as he chose his God over his son. But until this moment, Jonathan had not understood that he, too, was part of the story. Now he did.

Oh, Jesus! he cried out in despair and terror. *I am a child of Adam and Eve, too! I have sin, too. I am going to have to die for it!* None of this had occurred to him before!

He was dreadfully frightened. The bites of the serpents started to swell and burn, and his entire body trembled with pain and dread as he lay in the scorching sand—that scorching burning sand that was the color of bronze.

And he remembered the bronze serpent.

Hope flooded over him, and his panic subsided as he raised his head with the last of his strength to look up. If he could just see it!

There it was, lifted high atop a rocky hill. The bronze serpent was twisted around the pole, its tail stretching out to the left and its head to the right—in the shape of a cross.

The burning in his leg and arm and hand began to cool immediately as he gazed at it. He sighed in relief, but as he looked toward the serpent again, the hill became a pile of rocks, covered with the blood of Noah's sacrificed lamb.

The blood of an animal cannot take sin away, the voice reminded him.

The rocks began to blaze, and now a ram burned on them while the freed Isaac embraced his father.

But it reminded my Father of the Savior who would come someday who could take sin away . . .

Abraham and Isaac began to fade from sight. A doorframe, streaked with blood, stretched itself out over the hill, which had taken on the appearance of a glaring skull.

As the blood streaked toward the ground, it stained a rough-hewn wooden timber. A man hung on it, his hands stretched out to touch the blood on either side of the door. Then the door melted away, and only the hill, the cross, the dying man, and the blood remained.

Jonathan recognized the crown of thorns.

Now I know, he thought. *I know what caused the scars on Jesus' forehead. I know how he got those scars on his hands.*

The familiar voice spoke softly in his ear. *Jonathan,* it said, *do you understand now?*

He continued to watch, unable to answer. The voice spoke again, patiently repeating, *The blood of an animal cannot take sin away, but it reminded my Father of the Savior that would come someday who could take sin away . . .*

Jonathan, Jonathan—do you understand now?

The dream dissolved as Jonathan sat straight up in his bed. "*You're* the Savior!" he cried incredulously. "Oh, Jesus, yes—yes, I do understand!"

He scrambled to his feet. It all made sense now. How wonderful it was!

It was very early and the sun was not yet up, but Jonathan did not care. "Mary!" he cried out. "Mary, wake up! Something wonderful has happened!" He hurried over to wake her, but she was gone. The house was empty, and the jars she had set by the door were missing, too.

Jonathan ran out into the street. It was still dark—only the faintest light of dawn gleamed in the eastern sky. "Mary!" he shouted. "Where are you? Wait for me!" Again, no one answered him. But Jonathan knew where she must have gone, and he hurried toward the garden tomb.

He had run only a few steps when he saw a bright star suddenly leave the ranks of heaven and descend grandly to earth. Jonathan had almost reached the garden when it landed directly ahead of him, and the ground trembled violently. But this earthquake ended as quickly as it started, and Jonathan quickly regained his balance and raced on.

The first rays of dawn were rising as Jonathan found the angel standing at the door of the tomb. He was dressed in gleaming white, and shone like lightning. Jonathan recognized him as the leader of the heavenly armies that Jesus had shown him. Without a word, the angel put his shoulder against the enormous stone that covered the door of the tomb and rolled it away. Then he stood aside and waited.

The black opening chiseled in the rock gaped open now. Jonathan could not see inside from where he stood, and he was trembling with anticipation. But even when Jesus had been at his side, he had been a little afraid of this shining creature, and he dared not approach him now.

When he heard the voices of approaching women a moment later, Jonathan turned and ran toward them, hoping to find Mary.

He was so excited by now that he was at first surprised by the women's heavy grief. Some of them were weeping, but most were silent in their mourning, their eyes hollow and empty. As Jonathan had hoped, Mary was among them, carrying her jars with her, but she was speaking to one of the other women and did not see him. "How will we ever move that stone?" she was wondering bitterly. "It must be . . . "

At that instant, they entered the garden and saw the open tomb. The angel was no longer there, and Mary was so startled to see the stone already moved that she dropped her jars. Several of them broke, releasing a rich bitter fragrance into the morning.

She did not stop to pick up the jars but hurried with the other women to the gaping hole in the rock. Finding courage in theirs, Jonathan followed them and peeked inside after Mary went in.

Her voice echoed flatly in the little room. "He's *gone!*" she shrieked in despair. "Look!" She pointed to the linen shell that had wrapped the body. The cloth that had covered Jesus' head was set aside by itself and folded up. She snatched it up angrily. "He's gone!" she shouted hoarsely. "They've taken him!"

Then she turned, and gasped in fright as she saw the angel sitting quietly behind her. But before the angel could speak, she backed out of the tomb and into the growing light. The other women had seen him, too. For an instant, no one said anything. Then one of the older ones whispered to Mary, tight-lipped and fearful, "Go get Peter. Hurry!"

Mary hesitated, looked fearfully toward the open tomb and the empty linen wrappings, then ran away.

"Wait!" Jonathan called. He wanted to comfort

her, to tell her that everything was going to be all right. Something wonderful—he was not sure just what—was about to happen.

He leaped onto the path, running after her. "He had scars in his hands when *I* saw him!" the boy shouted after her. "How can he be dead when I've already seen him with the scars?"

But she was gone.

When he turned back to the garden, there were two angels standing there. The women were stricken with terror, but one of the angels said, "Don't be afraid. We know that you're looking for Jesus, who was crucified. Why are you looking for him among the dead? He is not here—he has risen!"

The women stared at them, speechless.

Finally, one of them whispered, *"He is alive?"*

The other angel smiled as he answered, "Don't you remember what he said to you while he was with you in Galilee? He said that he must be delivered into the hands of sinful men and be crucified, and on the third day he would rise again."

"Yes," one of the women murmured to herself. "He did say that."

"He did?" said another.

"Yes!" said a third, "I remember now."

The angel beckoned to them. "Come here," he continued. "Look at the place where they laid him."

They hesitantly approached him and again gazed with wonder into the empty tomb.

"Now hurry," instructed the angel. "Tell his disciples that he is alive and will meet them in Galilee."

Trembling and bewildered, the women fled away

from the tomb. Jonathan thought that they looked afraid and terribly happy all at the same time.

What now? he wondered. He did not know quite what to do. He wanted to follow them, but he wanted to see Jesus again, too. After a moment of hesitation, he saw Mary returning, so he waited for her.

She had not heard the angels' words and approached the tomb like one who had been utterly defeated. She was exhausted, and her walk said that she cared about nothing any more. She had already cried until she had no tears left, but still she sobbed brokenly. Jonathan had never seen anyone so unhappy.

When Mary reached the tomb, she looked inside again. The two angels were sitting there beside the empty linens. Before she could react, one of them asked her, "Why are you crying?"

This time, she stood her ground, but there was still fear in her voice as she answered in a broken, accusing tone, "They have taken my Lord away. I don't know where they have put him . . . "

She took a step backwards and almost collided with a man standing there. He asked her the same gentle question. "Why are you crying? Who are you looking for?"

For a moment she looked hopeful. "Are you the gardener?" she demanded tearfully, her voice rising in desperation. "Did you see who took him? Where is he? Wait! Did *you* take him? Just tell me where he is, and I will get him!"

Then the man smiled at her. "Mary!" he said.

Jonathan leapt to his feet as he suddenly recognized the voice.

Mary stared, too. "Teacher!" she cried out in astonishment. Fear and awe and love and joy passed over her face all at the same instant. "It is *you*," she whispered, reaching out for him.

But he backed away from her. "No," he said gently, "Don't cling to me—I have not returned to my Father yet."

Still she stared. "It *is* you," she said again, as if to convince herself.

"Yes," he said reassuringly, holding out his scarred hands for her to see. "But the others will want to know, too. Go tell Peter and John and the others that you have seen me. Tell them that I said, 'I am returning to my Father and your Father, to my God and your God.'"

She did not move, afraid to take her eyes off him.

"Go," he encouraged her gently. "They will be so glad to hear."

She took one step toward the garden gate, unable to tear herself away. "But," she stammered, "will I see you again?"

"Mary," he said, in the kindest voice imaginable, "you will be with me forever."

Praise, my soul, the King of heaven!
To His feet thy tribute bring;
Ransomed, healed, restored, forgiven—
Evermore His praises sing!
    Alleluia! Alleluia!
    Praise the everlasting King!

Angels in the heights, adore Him—
Ye behold Him face to face;
Saints triumphant, bow before Him,
Gathered in from every race.
    Alleluia! Alleluia!
    Praise with us the God of Grace!

Henry F. Lyte
based on Psalm 103

11

A Promise for Jonathan

Jonathan did not see Mary as she hurried away to find her friends and report the wonderful news. His eyes were flooded with tears, and Mary and the garden and the empty tomb all dissolved in a watery blur.

But Jesus did not. As old Jerusalem washed back into the past and the colors of the garden faded into a white mist, Jesus—the man who was God, the eternal Creator, the mighty power of Israel who was stronger even than death but who came on a summer night to claim a little handicapped boy for his own—stood tall and clear and bright and brilliant in front of him. Nothing else was real. There was only himself and Jesus as the world melted away around them.

Amidst the thick clouds, in the shining presence of the Lord, Jonathan found his voice again. "Will I be with you forever, too?" he asked quietly.

"That depends," Jesus replied. "You have a choice to make."

He held out his hands, and Jonathan came to him. This time, the little boy looked closely and solemnly at the deep scars. The question that had been burning in his mind could be voiced in a single word.

"Why?" Jonathan asked.

"Jonathan," Jesus said in reply, "Do you remember Noah?"

"Yes," Jonathan nodded.

"The little lamb died in his place so that he could live," Jesus explained again. "But remember what I told you—it is impossible for the blood of animals to take away sins."

Jonathan remembered. "But it reminded you of the Savior who could . . . " Carefully, he traced the marks the nails had left in Jesus' hands. The echoes of the hammer blows still rang clearly in his memory. He was suddenly filled with shame and could not bring himself to look into Jesus' eyes as he asked in a timid whisper, "That was *you*, wasn't it?"

Jesus knelt down and took the child's face in his hands. Jonathan wanted to look away, but he found that the love in his friend's face was too beautiful to resist. So he gazed helplessly into the light, his tears spilling down his cheeks as Jesus replied.

"Yes, Jonathan," he said gently. "*I* am that Savior. I am the perfect sacrifice—the lamb that God Himself provided for you—and my blood *can* take away your sin. And once your sin is gone, you can be with me.

"I died in your place—for *you*, Jonathan—so now you can live. Forever. With me."

Jonathan's heart ached with joy at these words, but he still struggled with confusion and could not speak.

That depends, Jesus had said.

Depends on what? Jonathan wondered. A gnawing

apprehension threatened his joy. *What do I have to do? What if it's too hard? What if . . .*

What if I can't do it?!

But as Jonathan looked into Jesus' eyes, the boundless love he found there seemed to reach deep within him, casting aside the pain and washing him with bright joy.

He felt the strength of the hands that were gently wiping the tears from his face, and he remembered that these were the hands that had commanded the oceans and had sculpted the faces of angels. And as he remembered, a ray of peace began to soothe his heart.

"Tell me what to do, Lord," he begged. "I'll do anything you say—anything at all. Just tell me! I could never, *never* bear to be apart from you!"

There was great love and tenderness in Jesus' reply. "Jonathan," he said, "do you remember Abraham?"

"Yes," Jonathan said.

"Abraham loved me so much that he was willing to give me his only son. In the same way, my Father loves *you* so much that He sent me, *His* only Son, to pay the penalty for your sin. That penalty is death—it didn't change. But *I* paid it *for* you. You don't have to pay it. You don't have to die yourself."

"I don't?"

"No."

"But . . . but what *do* I have to do?"

"Do you remember Moses?" Jesus answered.

"Yes."

"When he lifted up the bronze serpent in the desert, anyone who believed him and looked up at it would be cured of his deadly snake bite and would live.

"At the cross," he continued, "I was lifted up in the same way. So now, anyone who believes *me* and looks to *me* will be cured of his sin and will have everlasting life."

"Anyone who believes?" Jonathan murmured.

"Anyone!" Jesus said. "Jonathan, don't you understand yet? If you believe me, and trust me to do it, *I will take your sin away*. And you will have life with me that lasts forever!"

"But Jesus," Jonathan said incredulously, "I *do* believe you! I *want* you to take my sin away!"

Jesus took the little boy into his arms and kissed him. "Then," he said, "you will be with me forever!"

It was too simple. "That's it?!" Jonathan said in surprise. "Just believe you? Don't I have to do anything else?"

His friend's voice was gentle. "What else do you think you could do?" he asked.

Jonathan considered this. *What could I do? I could do nothing on my own when Jesus was not with me.* He could not sit up, or walk, or speak, or feed himself. He had to trust his family for *everything*. In fact, he would quickly die without their help.

But he was so different from other people. Maybe his brothers and sisters could do something. They could talk and run and sing and play the piano and even read the Bible . . .

But no, he decided. If the great floods of heaven could not wash away sin, what could *they* do? If the death of an innocent, sinless lamb could not pay the penalty for their sin, what could *they* offer—they who were born children of Adam and Eve, with sin already in them? If it took the violent death of the perfect

Creator God to take away sin, what was there that *anyone* could do?

"I can't do anything, Jesus," he said finally. "There isn't anything at all. You'll have to do it for me."

"I have already," Jesus replied. "Your sin is gone, Jonathan—gone forever. And now no one can *ever* take you away from me!"

"Never?" Jonathan was almost afraid to breathe. He had to be absolutely sure. "I'll *always* be with you?"

There was no hesitation at all in Jesus' voice as he replied—only firm, unshakable assurance. "Yes, Jonathan. Forever!"

And as he spoke, Jonathan heard again that commanding voice that had brought the stars leaping into existence. But this also was the voice of his friend who loved him, the voice he would hear forever.

He knew it now. He believed it! He was *free*!

A great space seemed to open up inside him, lightening as all the remaining fear in his heart melted away. But even as it emptied, his soul was poured full again—full to overflowing—with a flood of peace and hope, gladness and excitement. And love—such love as he could never describe!

He leaned his head back and shouted with laughter. *Forever!* The promise echoed repeatedly in his mind. *Forever! Forever!* He could not contain his gladness! He was bursting with joy and trembling with thanksgiving. But still it kept coming, welling up within him until he was sure he could not hold any more.

So Jonathan threw his arms around his friend, and Jesus gathered him tightly to himself. He, too, was laughing with Jonathan in joyous triumph. Neither of them spoke a word—there *were* no words! But Jonathan knew somehow that they were both giving thanks in their hearts to the Father of heaven for all His great gifts—Jonathan for Jesus, and Jesus for Jonathan.

At last Jonathan loosened his embrace, and Jesus set him down on his feet again. Jonathan ached from laughing so long, but he was warm and glad inside, and bursting with life.

"I've never been so happy!" he exclaimed. "Am I going to come live with you now?"

"Not for a while," Jesus replied. "I want you to stay with your family for now. But I will come back for you."

"And then what?" Jonathan asked. He motioned to the thick mists around him. "Will we come here again?"

"I will bring you to my Father's house," Jesus said. "Where there are many *wonderful* places to live. I have already started to prepare a very special place just for you, and when it is ready, I will come back for you, and take you there."

Jonathan was enthralled. "Where is it?" he wanted to know. "Can I see it?"

"Not right now," Jesus answered. "But you know the way to get there, so you *will* see it someday."

Jonathan was surprised. "But I don't know where it is! How could I know how to get there?"

Jesus smiled. "Because you know me. *I* am the way to my Father. No one ever comes to Him, except through me."

Jonathan considered all of this. "Will Mommy and Daddy be there, too?" he asked.

"Yes. And your brothers and sisters. And your grandma. And many other people who love you very much."

Jonathan took a deep breath before timidly asking his next question. "When I get there, will you let me talk and run and play, like I have while I've been with you?"

Jesus stood up. "Jonathan," he said with great tenderness, "I want you to meet someone."

Even as he spoke, Jonathan could see two figures approaching them through the white mist. One was an angel—Jonathan immediately recognized his tall, stern stature and shining robes. But the other was smaller, and as they drew near, Jonathan saw that he was a child about his own age.

But what a beautiful child! Jonathan had always thought that no one else in the world could be as beautiful as Kim and Matt and Jill and Mark. They were, he was certain, the most wonderful children ever!

But this boy was *perfect*. His clothes were as white as the angel's, and his golden face shone with light and joy. He was tall and confident, and when he saw Jesus, he left the angel's side and ran to him with effortless grace, laughing and greeting him with delight.

"You're back!" he cried joyously. "I'm so glad!"

Jonathan felt a twinge of jealousy as Jesus embraced and kissed the other boy lovingly, then whispered something to him that Jonathan could not hear. The boy answered him with a radiant smile.

Then Jesus pointed to Jonathan.

The boy was visibly surprised and gave Jesus a questioning look.

"Who's that?" he asked. Jesus said nothing. For a moment, the two children stared at each other in silent curiosity.

Jonathan was flushed. His perfect happiness of a moment ago was swept away by a sudden cloud of embarrassment and uncertainty. Although Jesus had let him stand and walk and speak for a while, he knew that he was still different. And now, next to this perfect boy—this shining child who greeted the Creator of all things as he would his own father or brother—Jonathan felt awkward and clumsy. He touched his small head self-consciously, remembering his distorted features, and looked down unhappily at his short legs. Suddenly, he was sure that the sin of the entire human race was displayed in all its ugliness all over him, and he turned his face away in shame.

"Jonathan," Jesus' voice came, "do you know who this is?"

"No," Jonathan replied in a hushed voice, stealing another look at the boy. But the boy was no longer staring in confusion. As soon as Jesus spoke Jonathan's name, a strange look of recognition began to spread over his face.

"*Jonathan?*" the boy said, turning back to Jesus in delighted astonishment. "This is *Jonathan?!*"

"David," Jesus laughed, "don't you recognize your brother?"

Before Jonathan could decide what had happened, the other boy gave an elated squeal and threw his arms around him, almost knocking him over. The boy was laughing and hugging him and chattering at him all at once in a voice so full of excitement that Jonathan could hardly understand a word.

"Jonathan!" he cried. "Oh, Jonathan, I've always wanted to meet you! Jesus has told me all about you, and I've asked and asked and *asked* to see you. Are you going to stay here with us? No, no, of course you're not—not yet. Oh, Jonathan, I'm glad . . . I'm *so* glad! But what's wrong? Don't you know me? I'm David—David, your brother!"

Jonathan was very confused. "But I only have two brothers," he said uncertainly, "Matthew and Mark . . . "

"Oh, yes," David replied confidently. "I know all about them. And Kim and Jill. And Mother and Dad. And Grandma! Oh, I especially want to meet Grandma! Grandpa is here, too, you know with us— we spend so much time together—and he has told me all about her. He misses her terribly, even though he's very happy here, so she must be very special. How *wonderful* for you that you get to know all of them. I wish I did! I've never met them, although Jesus says I will someday. Since all of them know him, we will all live here together. I just can't wait! What are they like? Is Mother pretty? What is her name?"

Jonathan hesitated, thinking. "Mary," he said at last. "Her name is Mary, and she is very pretty. I think she is the most beautiful mother in the world."

"I know a Mary here," David bragged happily. "And she is beautiful, too. She lived on earth while Jesus was there. We're good friends!"

Jonathan was startled for a moment. But then he realized, *Of course. That makes sense. She would be here, too.*

"But I still don't understand," Jonathan said, looking to Jesus helplessly. "I only have two brothers."

"David is your brother, too," Jesus explained simply, "even though you don't remember him. But he is a very special brother—he is your identical twin."

"My what?"

"Identical twins are brothers or sisters that look just alike. You see, I made the two of you at the same time. I started with just one tiny baby inside your mother, then divided you into two—you and David. And since I made you both from the same baby, you looked exactly alike."

Jonathan looked at the perfect, beautiful David, then back at his own stunted body. "But we don't look *anything* alike," he said sadly. "He is so perfect, and when I'm not with you, I can't even walk!"

"Listen to me carefully," Jesus said. He sat down, lifted Jonathan on one knee, and set David on the other. Holding them both closely, he explained.

"You, Jonathan, are still living in your first body. That body belongs in the world—the world that is full of sin that I have been telling you about. But I have already given David his *new* body—one that has never had any sin in it and that will live forever."

"But you said you would take away my sin!" Jonathan protested.

"And I have," Jesus assured him. "When you come here to live with me and your brother David, you will have a body just as beautiful and as perfect as his. But for just a little while longer, you will stay in the world with the same body you have always had.

"But listen: Even though everything in that world— like this body of yours—is stained in some way with sin, my Father knows that I have taken your sins away already. So when He looks at *you*," he pointed to

Jonathan, "He sees a boy just as beautiful and perfect and sinless as *you* . . . ," he pointed to David. "In our eyes, you are truly twins. We see no difference in you at all."

"You mean," Jonathan said slowly, reaching out shyly to touch his brother's hand, "that someday I will look just like him?"

Jesus laughed. "You already do!" he said, "You just can't see it yet. But someday you will—and so will everybody else."

"But why is David here," Jonathan asked, "instead of at home with me, and Mommy and Daddy?"

"Because before you were born, I brought him here to be with me, and I left you with your parents to live with them."

"But why?" Jonathan persisted.

"Someday I will tell you why," Jesus said. "But for now, just remember this: to me, you are *this* beautiful."

He hugged them both. "Kiss your brother," he said to David. "It is time for me to take him home now."

David's eyes filled with tears as he embraced Jonathan. "So soon!" he protested. "I wish you could stay longer. There is so much to see, so much I could show you. I know you don't remember me, but I have missed you *so much* . . . "

Jonathan was teary, too. "I'll miss you, too, now," he promised. "Maybe it won't be too long before I come back . . . ?" His voice trailed off, and both boys looked at Jesus hopefully, their hands clasped tightly together as if they never intended to let each other go. "Please say that we can see each other again soon!"

"Soon," Jesus promised, "I won't say exactly when, but it will be soon enough."

The angel, who had been standing unnoticed in the background, stepped forward and held out his hand for David. Jesus took Jonathan in his arms.

"Wait!" David cried. "Are you taking him back to our mother? Right now?"

"Yes," Jesus replied.

"Oh, let me come, too, just for a moment!" David begged, throwing his arms around Jesus and burying his face in his robe. "Please let me see her! I won't ever ask again. Just let me come with you and Jonathan . . . just for a moment!"

"Oh, yes, Jesus, please?" Jonathan joined in. "Let him come! Just for a moment. Please?"

Jesus sighed, but he was smiling. Resting one hand on David's head while he held Jonathan in his other arm, he said, "All right."

As he spoke, the white mist around them began to fade away. As it lifted, it revealed the familiar walls of Jonathan's own room hiding behind it. Mary was still sleeping quietly in the big chair, looking rested now, and the first colors of morning were starting to peek through the window.

The last of the mist vanished, and the earth became solid beneath their feet. They could hear the faint sounds of early morning stirring around them.

David was trembling. "That's her?" he whispered to Jonathan.

"Yes," Jonathan said.

David approached the sleeping woman timidly, then glanced back at Jesus as if for permission. Jesus nodded.

The golden boy with the shining face reached out and stroked his mother's dark hair once, very softly. His cheeks were wet, and for once, he had nothing to say.

"She sings to me sometimes," Jonathan said quietly.

David nodded in reply, unable to speak. He stood there, just for a moment, gazing at her. Then he kissed her cheek shyly. "Thank you, Jesus," he whispered and went obediently to take the angel's outstretched hand.

"Good-bye, Jonathan," David said as they began to fade from view. "I love you, and I'll be waiting for you!"

"I love you, too, David!" Jonathan called after him. "And I won't ever forget you. Good-bye! Good-bye!"

Then his brother and the angel were gone.

Suddenly, Jonathan realized that he was very tired. Without a word, Jesus set him down in his mother's arms, kissed him, and turned to go.

As the little boy snuggled down with his head against his mother's chest, he understood that the wonderful gifts Jesus had shared with him were for that night alone. Already, he could feel his arms and back stiffening again, and he knew he would soon have to give back the borrowed voice, too. But a clear, calm joy had settled over his heart, and as he gazed up at his friend to ask one last question, there was no sadness in his voice at all.

"Why did you make me like this?" he asked curiously.

"I have very good reasons for everything I do," Jesus replied. "But I do not always tell my people—not even those who love me and trust me the most.

Someday, when you have come to live with me, I will explain some of these things to you. Will you trust me in the meantime?"

Finding that he could no longer answer, Jonathan nodded and smiled with love and trust in his eyes. Jesus kissed him again. Then he stepped out of the room and back to his Father's house.

For a moment, Jonathan could see it as the walls and ceiling of the room rolled back. Far above him and beyond the world was a magnificent place where a shining throne of light was the center of all things.

The throne rumbled with thunder and lightning, and billowing clouds hid the one who sat there. But a sparkling jeweled rainbow encircled it, and from beneath it stretched a calm crystal-clear sea.

All around stood the hosts of heaven. There were men on thrones, dressed in white and crowned with gold. Strange creatures with many eyes and six wings clustered nearby, calling out with untiring joy the praises of their holy God. And answering them came the surrounding voices of thousands upon ten thousands of bright angels, robed in clouds and singing to God with the most beautiful voices and melodies that Jonathan had ever heard.

But the voices of the answering chorus must have numbered in the millions, and Jonathan imagined that *every* created thing in heaven and earth must have added to it as it was lifted up in praise. For beyond the angels was an endless multitude of people—all robed in white and singing together.

Among them, Jonathan could clearly see the laughing David, lifted high on his grandfather's shoulders. And there was Mary Magdalene, radiant with beauty and her face now shining and joyful. Even the newly-created little girl was there, her eyes sparkling and her arms raised in worship, as Jonathan remembered. But now she stood tall and regal in the company of angels, a golden trumpet at her side and a pair of silvery wings on her back, adding her clear voice to the celestial choir with joyous abandon.

But if any of them saw him, they gave no notice. All their eyes were on Jesus, as He returned to them, once more robing Himself the glorious splendor of heaven.

For as Jesus stepped out of Jonathan's room, His white robes became as dazzling as searing lightning, and the sash around His chest flashed with pure gold. As His feet once more touched the streets of heaven, they glowed like polished bronze. His eyes blazed like fire. His hair became as white as snow, and He wore many crowns on His head. And His face, so bright before, now shone with the brilliance of the sun, so that Jonathan could no longer look directly at Him, and even the angels covered their faces with their wings.

But even as the King of kings took His place again at the right hand of that throne, the voice that came back to Jonathan through the indescribable majesty and glory of heaven was that of his friend.

"You will not see me for a while, Jonathan," He said, and His voice was full of all the love and kindness and laughter that Jonathan remembered. "But I will always watch over you and take care of you. And I will come back for you soon. I will bring you to the place in my Father's house that I am preparing for you, and I will give you a beautiful new body. Then you will sing with your family, run with the children, and soar with the angels. And you will live here with me forever.

"*Forever,*" He said again. "I promise!"

And as Jonathan closed his eyes against the ever-increasing brilliance that flooded the room from heaven, his mother stirred from her sleep. As the morning sunbeams streamed over them through the little window, she kissed him fondly. "Hello, Baby," she whispered. "Good morning!"

But Jonathan heard only the fading echo of that beautiful voice as it called after him . . .

"*Jonathan, I love you—I love you, Jonathan . . . I love you!*"

About the Illustrator

Steve Miller is a free-lance illustrator in the Dallas area. His art has appeared several times as story, cover, and centerfold illustrations in Christian magazines such as *Venture, Pockets*, and *The Church Musician*. He has also designed book covers and Bible character cards for Heritage Worldwide, Inc., and his illustrations are liberally represented in the curriculum of Accelerated Christian Education.

His larger works include two impressive paintings—*Morning Response* and *Creation in Symphony*—commissioned by the Creation Evidences Museum in Glen Rose, Texas.

Steve and his wife Donna have been married for seventeen years and have two children—Christy and Ben. The Millers have become close friends with the Klentzmans over the past two years, and Steve has based all of the drawings for this book on photographs of Jonathan and his family.

About the Title Character

Jonathan Klentzman, age five, is the fifth of six children in his family—Kim, Matt, Jill, Mark, Jonathan, and Andrew (who was born after the completion of this book). When his identical twin brother died in early pregnancy, poisoning the blood supply they both shared, Jonathan's further development was severely retarded. At birth, he was diagnosed as having cerebral palsy.

Today, although his body is about the right size for his age, his head is no larger than an infant's. Although recent therapy has offered new hope that Jonathan might in time be able to learn some muscle control and possibly even communicate with his family, he remains entirely helpless. He cannot sit up, stand, crawl, walk, eat solid food, feed himself, or talk. Until very recently, he could not even sleep alone because of the spasticity of his back and neck muscles, but had to be held by a parent or sibling throughout the night.

But despite his severe disabilities, Jonathan is an alert, happy, and loving child. And every one in his family regards him as a blessing from God—the love and acceptance they daily display is nothing short of inspirational to everyone who knows them. The family involves Jonathan in all their activities—including their growing music ministry to area churches, conferences, and camps. They openly and sincerely speak of the ways the Lord has blessed them through this different, but very significant and special little life.